Qur'āns

QUR'ĀNS

Books of Divine Encounter

KEITH E. SMALL

with Francesca Leoni

Bodleian Library
UNIVERSITY OF OXFORD

First published in 2015 by the Bodleian Library
Broad Street
Oxford OX1 3BG

www.bodleianshop.co.uk

ISBN 978 1 85124 256 6

Text © Keith E. Small, 2015
Images, unless specified, © Bodleian Library, University of Oxford, 2015

Cover design by Dot Little at the Bodleian Library
Designed and typeset in 12½ on 20 Jenson by illuminati, Grosmont
Printed and bound by Great Wall Printing Co. Ltd., Hong Kong
on 157 gsm Neo Matt

British Library Catalogue in Publishing Data
A CIP record of this publication is available from the British Library

Contents

A PICTORIAL HISTORY
OF THE QUR'ĀN

The great theophany of Islam is the Quran.

Frithjof Schuon

THIS VOLUME TRACES THE HISTORY OF THE QUR'ĀN AS A BOOK from its earliest representative manuscripts on parchment to those on paper in the nineteenth/thirteenth century, when mass printing started to dominate the production of Qur'āns (for dates, see p. 9 below). Taken together, the manuscripts shown here span almost thirteen centuries chronologically as well as three continents geographically. They represent some of the finest examples of Islamic book art as well as humble productions used for the personal devotions of the ordinary faithful.

In general, books of holy scripture are an attempt to capture for posterity the fleeting moment of wonder, of transcendental encounter and of daring innovation that creates a new movement and sets it on an independent trajectory in history. Along the way, the book of scripture itself comes to be defined by that movement—its form as a book to be read, recited, venerated and cherished. The text becomes a vehicle of expression for the hearts and minds of individuals and groups and for each new generation to interpret and apply to its needs, whether those needs are personal, communal, spiritual or political. Humanity has invested tremendous intellectual, creative and technical resources in books of scripture because they have provided essential foundations for religious beliefs, political ideologies, societies and even empires. They have had wealth and artistic effort lavished on their production, and in the process have become the most significant historical expressions of the art of the book. In auction houses mere single pages of ancient copies command prices in the millions of pounds. In museum collections they rightfully hold pride of place, and can take our breath away with the beauty and creativity evident in the vision and skill of their craftsmanship.

This is all especially true of Islam's book of scripture, the Qur'ān. Like no other religious book, the Arabic Qur'ān became the foundation for visual culture across all Islamic cultures. Its Arabic script has become the distinctive Arab contribution to Islamic art through the ages and a universal mark of Muslim cultural and political influence wherever Islam has spread.

Before going on to the story of the Qur'ān as a book, though, we should consider one more important issue. Behind the Qur'ān's story there has been a theological idea that has informed and propelled its artistic and technological trajectory down to our day. It is an idea that continues to make news whenever there is a story involving blasphemy or mistreatment of copies of the Qur'ān. It is an idea that informs all devotional and political use of the Qur'ān. This idea starts from the question behind all books of holy scripture: how does a non-temporal God reveal his words in time and space? That he does, and that his revelations have been gathered into books, are major claims of many world religions like Judaism, Christianity and Islam, to name just three. The question of *when* the Qur'ān became a text, while seeming to be a simple matter of history, became the most significant issue of theological debate within early Islam, and it also became political, consuming its theologians, politicians and caliphs for centuries. This question also set the direction of the Qur'ān's entire artistic development in book form starting within its first century of compilation.

To a believing Muslim, the question of when the Qur'ān became a text revolves around the nature of the words that Muhammad spoke back in the early 600s CE. Were they words uttered to people in a particular historical context—that is, divinely inspired human words? Or were they *eternal* words—divine words only, given to Muhammad from on high but uncreated in themselves and somehow partaking of Allah's eternal knowledge which Muhammad received and recited without change to his audience? Though the Qur'ān seems to present both views within its text, for various political, theological and textual reasons, by Islam's fourth century the second view, that they are eternal words, came to dominate most Muslim belief, and this situation continues today. Very early on, this claim of divinity for the words also came to be tied to the Qur'ān in book form, and started to find expression in the various arts used to assemble, beautify and contain its text. Calligraphy quickly became the main vehicle for conveying the glory, venerability and sanctity of the Qur'ān's text.

In Christianity, the eternal Word of God was identified with an eternal spiritual person who also took on a human nature and body, Jesus Christ, the 'Word of God made flesh'. Jesus Christ is the focal point for Christians 'to apprehend the point of intersection of the timeless / With time', in the words of T.S. Eliot. The Christian believer celebrates the intersection of the eternal with time in the ritual of the Lord's Supper, or Holy Communion, and in a personal relationship with God mediated through the indwelling Holy Spirit.

For Muslims, that point of intersection is the Qur'ān. In Islam, the eternal Word of God was identified with Divine Speech given to a human prophet, Muhammad, and gathered into a book, the Qur'ān. The believer seeks to experience that sacred intersection of the eternal with time in the experience of vocal Qur'ān recitation. One important written tradition attributed to Muhammad states:

> Someone who reads the Koran is as if he were talking to Me
> and I were talking with him.
>
> *Hadith Qudsi*

The Qur'ān in Arabic came to be the means of mediating the presence of God in the lives of Muslims, both personally and communally. This is why in Islam the Qur'ān is considered to be the Word of God only when it is in its Arabic written or spoken form, and translations are only considered interpretations. This is also why Muslims believe the Qur'ān must be experienced vocally and aurally in Arabic in order for the divine encounter to be fully realized. To Muslims, the Qur'ān is much more than a book, and over the centuries, as the examples in this volume show, scribes and artists have sought to have their art live up to the divine aspirations Muslim believers attach to the text.

Following a chronological outline, the first three chapters in this book present the history of the Qur'ān as a book, from the earliest simple parchment manuscripts to some of the finest examples of highly decorated paper Qur'āns. These examples throw light on a number of questions. Why were manuscripts originally portrait format, then switched to landscape format, and then back to portrait format again? How did illuminated decoration of the pages develop, first in parchment Qur'āns and then in paper ones? How did artistic trends in Qur'āns develop regionally concerning colours, intricacy and hidden spiritual meaning? How was the Qur'ān as a text and as a book modified to enhance the practice of oral recitation and memorization, especially in regard to the development of the precise spelling of Arabic letters?

The last three chapters take a topical approach. As the West discovered Islamic scholarship in the sixteenth/tenth and seventeenth/eleventh centuries, how did European and Islamic approaches to Qur'ān scholarship compare? How is the worldwide spread of Islam represented in the art of Qur'āns? How has the Qur'ān been used for personal devotion and spiritual protection through the centuries? The manuscripts presented here illuminate the issues raised by these key questions.

A NOTE ON THE COLLECTIONS

The Bodleian Library at Oxford University has been the central repository for research materials for the university for over 400 years. When the library opened to the public in 1602/1010 it had one Arabic manuscript, a Qur'ān, MS. Bodl. Or. 322 (featured in the fourth chapter). The library now possesses more than 2,500 individual Arabic manuscripts, 155 of which are Qur'āns or Qur'ān portions. Many were acquired by purchase or came in as bequests and individual gifts from alumni of Oxford University over the last four centuries—gifts from merchants, diplomats, scholars, clergymen, adventurers and soldiers, gratefully making a small return for the education they had received, and wanting to help uphold Oxford's reputation as a centre for excellence in Arabic and Middle Eastern studies. Some of the human stories behind the manuscripts are told in the course of this volume. This collection is also notable in that its treasures are not hidden away as part of a collector's private store. They are available for access as part of a working library. In all, they represent one of the most significant academic research collections for the study of the Qur'ān in the West.

The Ashmolean Museum in Oxford holds a small but meaningful group of Islamic works on parchment and paper that includes several Qur'ānic folios and a few codices. This material is part of the Islamic art collection of the Department of Eastern Art, which was established in 1961/1381 following the transfer of the Asian collections previously housed at the Museum of Eastern Art in the old Indian Institute of the university. With a few exceptions, the Qur'ānic material entered the Ashmolean in the last decade or so through gifts. Most notable amongst them was the recent Christopher T. Gandy bequest, which includes forty-two individual folios, a complete section from a thirty-volume Mamluk Qur'ān with its original flap-binding, and a fine, albeit incomplete, rebound Safavid single-volume Qur'ān. Taken together these works offer a representative selection of manuscript material from the most important artistic centres of the Islamic world between the eighth/second and the seventeenth/eleventh centuries, posing the conditions to pursue a more systematic acquisition of Qur'ānic material in order to establish a more faceted and historically significant survey. As is the case for the special collections of the Bodleian, the Ashmolean Museum offers direct access to its collections through the Jameel Study Centre, a facility established after the 2009/1430 refurbishment of the museum and available to the public for educational and research activities during regular museum hours. All of the manuscripts with shelfmarks beginning EA are from the collection of the Ashmolean Museum. Their captions were provided by Dr Francesca Leoni, the Yousef Jameel Curator of Islamic Art for the Ashmolean.

The David Collection in Copenhagen, Denmark has an extensive collection of Islamic art. They have kindly provided an image of a particularly significant page from what is perhaps the oldest Qur'ān manuscript in existence, featured in the next chapter. This manuscript provides the simple and unassuming starting point from which the Qur'ānic book tradition flowered into its exquisite and multiform diversity.

ON ARABIC TRANSLITERATION AND DATE CONVENTIONS

Romanization of Arabic titles and technical terms follow the Library of Congress system of transliteration. This system has been simplified for ease of reading with Arabic proper names. Dates are given according to both the Western CE and the Islamic AH calendars. It is done in the following manner: CE/AH—1602/1010; 1600s/1000s; 17th/11th century; seventeenth/eleventh century.

بسم الله الرحمن الرحيم ... الله ... محمد ... لا اله الا الله ... رسول ... المؤمنون ... المسلمين ... الحمد لله

FROM PREACHING
TO A DIVINE BOOK

W HEN DID THE QUR'ĀN START ITS LIFE AS A BOOK?
Current popular accounts present a simple story: Muhammad
received revelations during the twenty-three years of his prophetic career
between 610 and 632 CE. As he preached these revelations, they were written
down and collected, both in written forms and in memorized ones by his
followers. His immediate political successors, the 'rightly guided caliphs', took
measures to preserve these collections, and the third one, 'Uthman ibn 'Affan,
especially had a committee collate the written and the memorized versions into
an official edition for the use of the growing Muslim empire. This, in various
expanded versions, is often termed the 'traditional' view.

While there is truth in this story, when one looks at the earliest available
accounts in Islamic sources, it is also not that simple. The traditional view
is actually a relatively modern interpretation coming out of the late medieval
period that harmonizes older accounts which support a longer and more
complicated history of the process of the Qur'ān becoming a book. Also, today,
traditional religious views and scholarly critical views must live side by side

with a healthy openness to mutual questioning and self-correction. Historical discoveries are driving much of this. Modern manuscript studies, using ancient manuscripts like the ones pictured in this book, are recovering the more ancient history of the Qur'ān, confirming and expanding the full diversity of the history that one finds in the early Islamic historical sources and also placing that history within the broader cultural and social context of late Near Eastern antiquity. The manuscripts featured here cover the period from the Qur'ān's initial inscription to its becoming a clearly defined book of scripture. Though the major features of the content and order of its text were formalized within a century of Muhammad's death, many of the smaller features used for recitation, as well as the precise spelling of the text, took three centuries to complete.

While there is no stated Islamic ban against representational art in the Qur'ān itself, representational art has never been used in Qur'ān manuscripts as it was with other religious traditions. Artistic themes common in late Near Eastern antiquity were used under the Umayyads (661/40–750/132), but their successors, the Abbasids (750/132–1254/652), at first restricted ornamentation in Qur'āns, concentrating on the calligraphy of the text, perhaps as an indication of the weight being given to the sanctity of the divine words. However, within two centuries, other concerns became dominant—for a visually impressive and distinctive script that was an aid to accommodate various memorized versions of the Qur'ān and for the script to be a visual pointer to the theology consolidating around the Qur'ān, it being the immutable point of contact with the Divine. Ornamentation developed using strictly Islamic themes that increasingly served the liturgical needs of recitation together with theological aspects of the text.

A Qur'ānic palimpsest

This is a page from what might be the oldest Qur'ān manuscript in existence, perhaps from the mid- to late 600s. Its script style, called *hijazi*, was the ordinary Arabic script of the time used for business and administrative documents. It has the added interest of being a 'palimpsest'—an erased and rewritten manuscript. The first writing on the parchment was washed off and a second level was rewritten within a generation using the same script but a different portion of Qur'ānic text. The first level, showing light brown, contains the most significant textual variations ever found for the Qur'ān, with words and phrases different to the current version. The second level is very close to what is now considered the normal text, and was possibly written to replace the first level as part of an official editing project that Islamic tradition asserts occurred during the reigns of the early Islamic caliphs.

Inv. no. 86/2003, recto. The David Collection, Copenhagen (photograph: Pernille Klemp). Lower text: *Sūrat al-Baqarah* (The Cow), 2:106–217; 7th/1st century. Upper text: 2:277–282; 8th/2nd century.

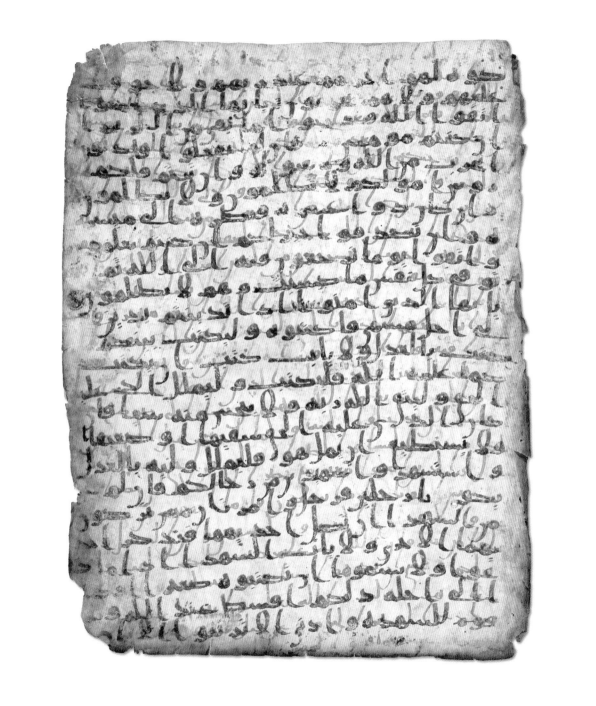

An early Abbasid page

During the Umayyad period, a script style known generally as *kufic* was refined into a special script for Qur'āns to set them apart from ordinary books. The Abbasids, the next great dynasty of Islamic rulers after the Umayyads, made this their main script style for Qur'āns. This page has a gold dot on the bottom line, which together with the gold letter *alif* presents a textual variant of significance in that it changes the word. It is at surah 17:64 in a section on the temptations from Satan. The gold letter allows the word to be read two ways. Without the *alif*, the reading in all Qur'āns today translates as 'your foot soldiers' or 'your infantry'; with the *alif*, it translates as 'your men'. Early scholars read it either way. In the upper left margin are ownership stamps and various librarian notes, possibly from the sixteenth/ninth to seventeenth/tenth centuries.

MS. Arab. c. 38 fol. 13r; *Sūrat al-Isrā'* (The Night Journey), 17:60–64; 8th/2nd century.

بِسْمِ اللَّهِ الرَّحْمَٰنِ الرَّحِيمِ

قَالَتْ إِنَّ الْمُلُوكَ إِذَا دَخَلُوا قَرْيَةً أَفْسَدُوهَا وَجَعَلُوا أَعِزَّةَ أَهْلِهَا أَذِلَّةً ۖ وَكَذَٰلِكَ يَفْعَلُونَ

وَإِنِّي مُرْسِلَةٌ إِلَيْهِم بِهَدِيَّةٍ فَنَاظِرَةٌ بِمَ يَرْجِعُ الْمُرْسَلُونَ

فَلَمَّا جَاءَ سُلَيْمَانَ قَالَ أَتُمِدُّونَنِ بِمَالٍ فَمَا آتَانِيَ اللَّهُ خَيْرٌ مِّمَّا آتَاكُم بَلْ أَنتُم بِهَدِيَّتِكُمْ تَفْرَحُونَ

An early fragment

Although severely damaged this folio gives us a glimpse of the unique quality of the codex of which it was once part. The script, characterized by an elegant horizontal stretching of the letters known as *mashq* and by crescent-shaped strokes for the letter *nun*, makes it comparable to other Qur'āns of this time. The script style also possesses a range of archaic features that have led scholars to associate the manuscript with an eighth/second-century date. The likelihood that the vowels, indicated by the red dots, and diacritical marks, presented as single, double or triple strokes, were a later addition reinforces this conclusion. The green dots match places where alternative Qur'ān readings attributed to one of Muhammad's prominent companions and Qur'ān reciters, 'Abd Allah ibn Mas'ud, would have been found. Other manuscripts use the green dots to note the voiced glottal stop written with the letter *hamza*.

EA2009.18 © Ashmolean Museum, University of Oxford. *Sūrat al-Anbiyā'* (The Prophets), 21:36–42; 8th/2nd century.

وهم بذكر الرحمن هم
كفرون خلق الانسن من عجل
سأوريكم ءايتي فلا
تستعجلون ويقولون متى هذا
الوعد ان كنتم صدقين
لو يعلم الذين كفروا حين
لا يكفون [illegible] جوههم النار
ولا عن [illegible] ولا هم ينصرون
بل تأتيهم بغتة فتبهتهم فلا
يستطيعون ردها ولا هم ينظرون
ولقد استهزئ برسل
من قبلك فحاق بالذين سخروا
منهم ما كانوا به يستهزءون
قل من يكلؤكم باليل
والنهار من الرحمن بل هم
عن ذكر ربهم معرضون

A later Abbasid page

This ninth/third-century parchment demonstrates further development of the Abbasid *kufic* script style and also a development to simplify the presentation of the text. In this era there seems to be a trend to distinguish fewer of the consonants than in earlier Abbasid manuscripts and even the prior Umayyad ones. The spacing between words and certain letters is increased, and certain letters are elongated. The red dots continue the practice for designating short vowels. One of the early caliphs is said to have required Qur'āns to be written in large letters, for which this script is ideally suited. Also, the main page format was shifted to landscape presentation, which allowed greater artistic possibilities for the script and also made the Qur'ān visually distinct from Christian and Jewish scriptures, a concern amidst the increasing religious and political contacts after the Islamic conquests during Islam's first centuries.

MS. Arab. c. 75 fol. 1v; *Sūrat al-Naml* (The Chapter of the Ants), 27:36–42; 9th/3rd century.

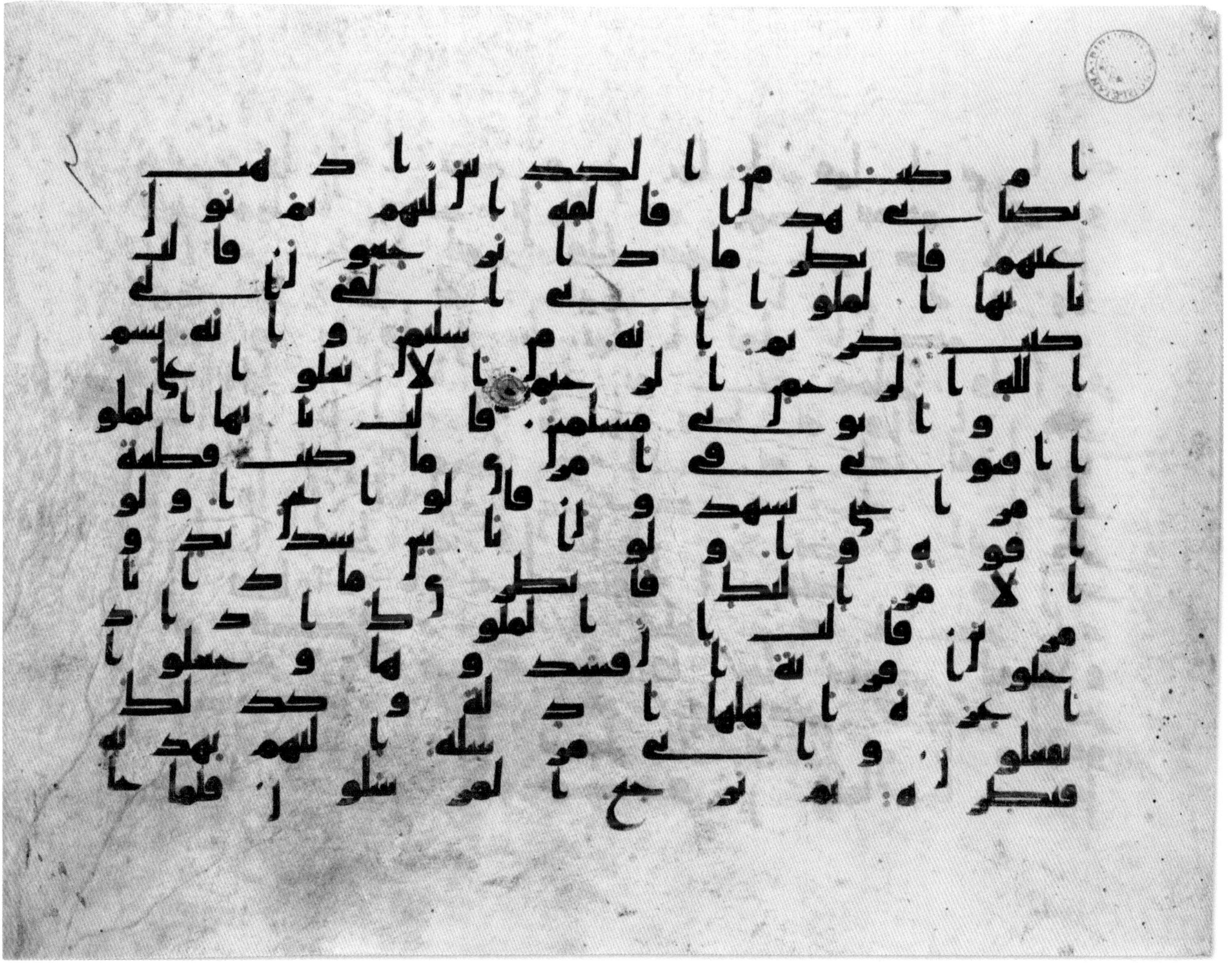

A page with later decoration

Additional development of the Abbasid style of script and the Abbasid style
of Qur'ān can be seen in this parchment page. While there are only minor
developments in letter forms, the lines are more carefully written in terms of
spacing between groups of letters and straightness of the lines. There are also
fewer lines per page, the introduction of a trend that was going to continue
for a couple of centuries. There are also green dots added to the red ones,
both added at a time later than the original inscription of the text. In this
manuscript the red dots signify short vowels and the green ones note the
glottal stop *hamza*. The simple coloured frame was probably added at a later
time, perhaps in sixteenth/tenth-century Safavid Persia (Iran). The text on
this page recounts part of the Qur'ān's version of the story of Mary residing
in the Jerusalem Temple.

MS. Arab. f. 3 fol. 2r; *Sūrat al-i-'Imrān* (The Family of Amran), 3:37–39; 9th/3rd century.

بسم الله الرحمن الرحيم

ا فا لـ مؤ مر محد ا لله لا

ذ ا لله بو د و قر ساو يسو حسا

ملبا د حا و حو ناو وه

فا ز د يهد لو مر لد نكا

د به طه با نكا سمع الد

عا فا د ها الملكه و هو

فا هذ يصطل في العبا يد

نا ر ا لله لسو كا يو محد

An elegant Abbasid leaf

This manuscript continues and extends the trends for elongation of the script and restriction of words and lines of text. There is a complete removal of the diacritical marks that distinguish consonants, making the script even more difficult to read. The scribe carefully aligned the letters of the right margin, and what are red dots in the prior manuscripts are in this one gold, with verse endings marked with little sun-like florets. The simple but elegant uses of black and gold further enhance the sanctity of the divine word, elevating it above the plane of ordinary writing and speech. At the time of the creation of this manuscript, the doctrine of the eternal, uncreated Qur'ān was becoming the majority view, and pages like this sought to provide a personal encounter with that ineffable realm with their abstract visual aspect tied to the reader's internalized memorized text.

MS. Arab. c. 38 fol. 16r; *Sūrat ar-Rahmān* (The Most Gracious), 55:8–10; 9th/3rd century.

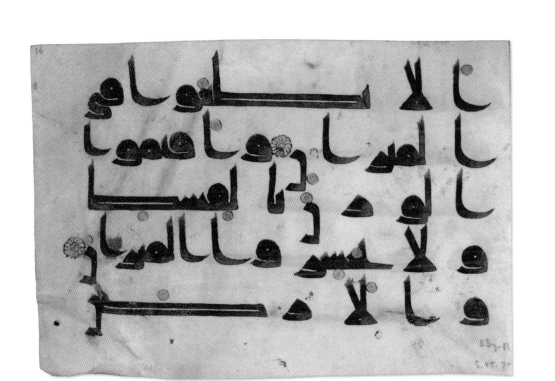

An illuminated surah title

As compared to Western styles of illumination, distinctly Islamic conventions can be seen in this manuscript. Instead of pictorial representation of authors or the content in chapters, Qurʾān illumination serves the functionality of the manuscript decorating features such as the titles of chapters, verse endings, groups of verses, and other readers' aids for use in private and public recitation. Ornate plant motifs like stylized palm branches marking the beginnings of surahs became popular, perhaps because of their resonance with the Qurʾān verse *Sūrat Ibrāhīm* 14:24 that compares the Qurʾān to a good tree with a firm root and branches in heaven. This particular box appears unfinished and gives clues as to how the artists would carefully construct their work. The names of surahs often come from a prominent word in the chapter, not necessarily from its content. This surah is named after a word that does not appear until its seventy-first verse.

MS. Marsh 178 fol. 33v, 34r; *Sūrat Ṣād* and *Sūrat az-Zumar* (The Groups), 38:88–39:1; 9th/3rd century.

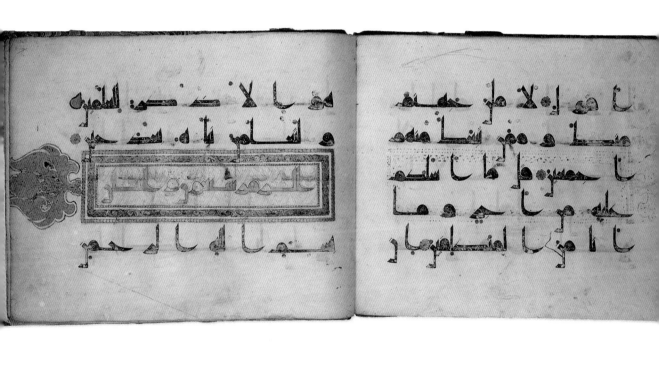

The Amajur Qur'ān

Early Qur'āns are especially difficult to date, as they rarely provide information such as the date or place of execution, or the name of the patron responsible for their realization. This bifolio is a rare exception. As indicated by an inscription on the top margin, it was endowed to a religious foundation by Amajur, governor of Damascus between 870/256 and 878/264. The bulk of the manuscript, which is today in Istanbul, contains further endowment notes recording the date of the donation, 876/262, and an indication of the place to which it was destined, Tyre in modern Lebanon, without however mentioning the specific institution. The size of the script, spaciously arranged in three lines per page, tells us that a considerable effort and expense went into the production of this manuscript. Scholars have estimated that, when finished, this multi-volume codex contained over 6,400 folios.

EA1996.54 © Ashmolean Museum, University of Oxford. *Sūrat al-i-'Imrān* (The Family of Amram), 3:55 and 3:57; late 9th/3rd century.

A leaf with a holy attribution

This beautiful Abbasid parchment page was recently and unexpectedly discovered bound in with two seventeenth/eleventh century Persian treatises on calligraphy. The gold frame and wash were probably added during the sixteenth/tenth-century Persian Safavid dynasty (Iran), known for collecting and decorating ancient Qur'ān manuscripts. This leaf has a Persian inscription attributing the script to the sixth Imam of the Twelver Shi'ites, Ja'far al-Sadiq (d. 765/148), a highly revered religious figure thought also to have been a master calligrapher, but the attribution is probably mistaken because the script style is one developed later than his era. Ancient manuscripts with attributions of early religious leaders have been used throughout Islamic history to enhance religious and political credentials. Also, Qur'ānic calligraphy is believed by many Muslims to have begun with Muhammad's son-in-law, 'Ali ibn Abi Talib, who is held to be the first Imam in the line of the twelve Shi'ite Imams.

MS. Fraser 48; *Sūrat Ṣād*, 38:8–12; 10th/4th century.

A page with a prostration symbol

This simple Abbasid parchment page emphasizes the sanctity of the words of the Qur'ān in two particular ways. One is in the way the lines of script are written carefully in their measured, elongated, dignified script, with the number of words per line and the lines per page both restricted. The second way is with the gold marginal note tied in with the gold circle at the end of surah 13:15 in line 4. This is an additional aid to recitation, a 'prostration' or *sajdah* reminder. There are fourteen places in the Qur'ān where a pious Muslim is to pause and prostrate. This note in a tenth/fourth-century manuscript highlights the antiquity of this practice among Muslims. Surah 13:15 proclaims that all in heaven and earth should submit to Allah alone—a fitting place for a believer to prostrate. The page was acquired by the Bodleian in 1714/1126.

MS. Marsh 2 fol. 7v; *Sūrat al-Ra'd* (The Thunder), 13:15–16; 10th/4th century.

بسم الله الرحمن الرحيم
سبحان الذي اسرى بعبده

THE TRANSITION
FROM PARCHMENT
TO PAPER

I do not know of any other form of writing in which the letters undergo so much beautifying and refining as they do in Arabic writing.

Ya'qub b. Ishaq al-Kindi (d. 873/260)

T HE PREVIOUS CHAPTER HAS SHOWN THE RAPID DEVELOPMENT of Arabic script from a practical hand to an ornamental script of power and dignity, fit for a book proclaimed to be the Book of God. This chapter documents a development of the script in the direction of elegance, beauty and refinement. And this refinement of script was accompanied by the development of ornamental arts as they were applied to Qur'āns. Compared to the scripts used in other religious texts in this period, perhaps no other book of sacred scripture went through such rapid development to beautify the appearance of the words themselves and develop the text into a vehicle held to be in some way mediating the presence of God.

The manuscripts presented here also document transitions from the use of parchment to paper, and from a landscape page format back to a portrait one. There was also the development of dramatically increased literacy in

Islamic domains as Arabic became the language of empire. Though books were still expensive, the use of paper made them more affordable.

Spelling improvements that had been made in the administrative chancelleries were introduced into Qur'āns, which meant that the ambiguities that the former coloured dot systems tried to address were no longer a problem. The Arabic script in Qur'āns could precisely represent exactly what was spoken and heard. With these improvements, by about 1000 CE, ten slightly different ways of reciting the Qur'ān (with some slight differences of meaning involved) gained recognition and acceptance and were recorded in manuscripts. These ten were named after prominent early Qur'ān reciters and some of them came in the following centuries to have regional popularity.

One final development was that there was consolidation around the theological view that the Qur'ān was somehow in its essence an eternal text, related to Allah's eternal attribute of knowledge. The relationships of the Qur'ān on its eternal tablet to Allah himself and to the physical manifestations of the Qur'ān in this world were never completely harmonized, and were left as spiritual beliefs to be held by faith. These beliefs, however, had a profound effect on the art of the book in that the physical Qur'āns came unequivocally to share in the metaphysical aura associated with the Divine Presence of Allah. Qur'āns became holy objects in and of themselves, and the act of producing them became a spiritual, meritorious act, requiring the scribe to be ritually pure and conferring blessings upon the scribe, the patron and those who would gaze on the finished Qur'āns.

An early paper Qur'ān

One of the earliest paper Qur'āns in existence, this manuscript has many rare features. It is in a transitional script style approaching what many call 'eastern *kufic*' but is more technically referred to as the 'new style'. This manuscript combines the large letter size of earlier manuscripts with a newer angular script style that rapidly developed into a regional specialty. It dates to the early 900s/300s, shortly after paper had been introduced to Islamic lands while parchment was still the preferred material for Qur'āns. It uses an archaic system for spelling the Arabic letters for *f* and *q*. It also has a rare example of an alternative surah title *Subḥāna*, 'Praise', instead of *al-Isrā*, 'The Night Journey'. The illumination was added much later by pasting it in. This was possibly done to make it more attractive to a collector. It was purchased in Iran in the 1920s/1340s, and was rebound with its pages out of order.

MS. Arab. e. 179 fols 6v, 7r; *Sūrat al-Isrā'* (The Night Journey), 17:1 and 17:15–18; 10th/4th century.

بسم الله الرحمن الرحيم
سبحان الذى اسرى بعبده

A new-style Qur'ān

This fragmentary portion of the Qur'ān was refurbished in the course of its history. The pages were reformatted using paper from both the original codex and additional strips, especially for the lower edge, and an interlinear Persian translation was added. The distinctive script, characterized by bold strokes varying in thickness that highlight the vertical shafts of some letters as well as the tails of the ones falling underneath the baseline, received several additional names, including eastern *kufic*, Persian *kufic* and broken cursive. Like other scribal hands, including *maghribi* and *naskh*, the new style was part of the transformation begun during the tenth/fourth and eleventh/fifth centuries, leading to a gradual refinement of round scripts, used for administrative purposes until then, to make them suitable for transcribing the holy book. This manuscript represents a transitional period with the large letters echoing the older tradition, though with a more refined script.

EA2009.19 fol. 30v, 31r, © Ashmolean Museum, University of Oxford. *Sūrat Muḥammad*, 47:78 through *Sūrat al-Fatḥ* (The Victory), 48:3; 11th/5th–12th/6th century.

يَسْتَبْدِلْ قَوْمًا غَيْرَكُمْ

ثُمَّ لَا يَكُونُوا أَمْثَالَكُمْ

سورة الفتح مدنية وهي تسع وعشرون آية

بِسْمِ اللَّهِ الرَّحْمَٰنِ الرَّحِيمِ

إِنَّا فَتَحْنَا لَكَ فَتْحًا مُبِينًا

لِيَغْفِرَ لَكَ اللَّهُ مَا تَقَدَّمَ

مِنْ ذَنْبِكَ وَمَا تَأَخَّرَ وَ

يُتِمَّ نِعْمَتَهُ عَلَيْكَ وَيَهْ

دِيَكَ صِرَاطًا مُسْتَقِي

مًا وَيَنْصُرَكَ اللَّهُ نَصْرًا

A refined new-style folio

This is one of eight folios originating from a rare manuscript of the Qur'ān which combines Arabic verses with a Persian translation and commentary. Although Arabic is the language in which the Qur'ān was revealed—and the only one accepted for its recitation—translations and commentaries in both Persian and Turkish increased from the twelfth/sixth century onwards. These allowed not only for better understanding of the text, but also for the spread of Islam's principles in areas where Arabic was not the main language. Their presence along with the original Arabic is an indication of Islam's deeper penetration in the eastern areas of the caliphate at this time. Note the change to a vertical page format, a trend that would now be almost universal in Qur'āns. The script style is representative of the heights achieved for this script for conveying the dignity and sanctity of the word of God.

An Andalusian page

Unlike the rest of the Islamic world, where paper became the preferred medium for the production of Qur'āns from the eleventh/fifth century on, North Africa and Spain continued to copy the revelation on parchment well into the fifteenth/ninth century. The squarish page format is a further characteristic of codices realized in the western Islamic lands. The same can be said for the employment of the rounded *maghribi* script whose development is traditionally associated with Maghreb (North Africa) and found in relation to the luxury book production of this region as well as Muslim Spain. Round scripts and the full use of vowels made the text more legible, as seen here. This page also contains illuminated verse divisions, in the form of gold knots, and marginal decorations, in the form of drop-shaped and round medallions. These are generally used to indicate a five- and ten-verse sequence respectively.

EA1993.395, © Ashmolean Museum, University of Oxford. *Sūrat 'Abasa* (He frowned), 80:32–38; 13th/7th century.

الإنسان إلى كعامه

إنا صببنا الماء صبا

ثم شققنا الأرض شقا

فأنبتنا فيها حبا وعنبا

وقضبا وزيتونا

ونخلا وحدائق غلبا

وفاكهة وأبا متاعا

A Tunisian
maghribi-style page

This sixteenth/tenth century manuscript is unique among *maghribi* script-style Qur'āns, and extremely rare among Qur'āns in general, in that the text is inscribed in blue ink. One page from the same manuscript is in the collection of the State Archive of Vienna (Orientalische Handschriften, n. 593), which is thought to have originally been the property of one of the Ottoman client rulers, the Bey of Tunis. The only other blue ink Qur'āns are a few Ottoman Qur'āns in *naskh* script style from this era. This page has a mix of Eastern and Western Islamic writing and decoration styles. The gold verse markers show continuity of style with the earlier Western tradition, while symbols like *shadda* and *hamza* are in line with Eastern conventions. The title in gold also shows Eastern influence in the way *f* is distinguished from *q*, which is different from the Western manner found in the text.

MS. Pococke 444 fol. 1v; *Sūrat Saba'* (Sheba), 34:1–8; 16th/10th century.

بسم الله الرحمـ ن الرحيم

الحمد لله الذي له ما في السموات وما في الأرض

وله الحمد في الآخرة وهو الحكيم الخبير ۝ يعلم

ما يلج في الأرض وما يخرج منها وما ينزل من السماء

وما يعرج فيها وهو الرحيم الغفور ۝ وقال الذين

كفروا لا تأتينا الساعة قل بلى وربي لتأتينكم

عالم الغيب لا يعزب عنه مثقال ذرة في السموات ولا

في الأرض ولا أصغر من ذلك ولا أكبر إلا

في كتاب مبين ۝ ليجزي الذين آمنوا وعملوا الصالحات

أولئك لهم مغفرة ورزق كريم ۝ والذين سعوا

في آياتنا معاجزين أولئك لهم عذاب من رجز أليم ۝ ويرى

الذين أوتوا العلم الذي أنزل إليك من ربك هو الحق

ويهدي إلى صراط العزيز الحميد ۝ وقال

الذين كفروا هل ندلكم على رجل ينبئكم إذا

مزقتم كل ممزق إنكم لفي خلق جديد ۝ أفترى

A leaf in elegant *muhaqqaq* script

This single page is from a Qur'ān that could have been produced between the thirteenth/seventh and fifteenth/ninth centuries. Its script is an elegant, sweeping rounded style called *muhaqqaq*, which became the Qur'ān script style of choice in these centuries in the east, replacing the angular new style. This style is one of six decorative scripts that were developed from the rounded utilitarian cursive scripts used in the administrative work of the chancelleries. The other five are: *thuluth*, *rayhani*, *naskh*, *riqa'* and *tawqi'*. These 'six scripts' came to be celebrated for their artistic merit and were used for inscribing books of many types. *Muhaqqaq* became the script *par excellence* for Qur'āns, with some of the others being used for surah titles or occasionally for the text. One feature of this page that preserves vestiges of textual fluidity from the earlier era is that the verse numbering system is different from current Qur'āns.

MS. Bodl. Or. 163 fol. 1r; *Sūrat ash-Shūra* (The Consultation), 42:16–21; 13th/7th–15th/9th century.

وَلَهُمْ عَذَابٌ شَدِيدٌ ۞ اللَّهُ الَّذِي أَنْزَلَ الْكِتَابَ بِالْحَقِّ وَالْمِيزَانَ

وَمَا يُدْرِيكَ لَعَلَّ السَّاعَةَ قَرِيبٌ يَسْتَعْجِلُ بِهَا الَّذِينَ لَا يُؤْمِنُونَ بِهَا

وَالَّذِينَ آمَنُوا مُشْفِقُونَ مِنْهَا وَيَعْلَمُونَ أَنَّهَا الْحَقُّ أَلَا إِنَّ الَّذِينَ يُمَارُونَ

فِي السَّاعَةِ لَفِي ضَلَالٍ بَعِيدٍ ۞ اللَّهُ لَطِيفٌ بِعِبَادِهِ يَرْزُقُ مَنْ يَشَاءُ

وَهُوَ الْقَوِيُّ الْعَزِيزُ ۞ مَنْ كَانَ يُرِيدُ حَرْثَ الْآخِرَةِ نَزِدْ لَهُ فِي حَرْثِهِ

وَمَنْ كَانَ يُرِيدُ حَرْثَ الدُّنْيَا نُؤْتِهِ مِنْهَا وَمَا لَهُ فِي الْآخِرَةِ مِنْ نَصِيبٍ

أَمْ لَهُمْ شُرَكَاءُ شَرَعُوا لَهُمْ مِنَ الدِّينِ مَا لَمْ يَأْذَنْ بِهِ اللَّهُ وَلَوْلَا كَلِمَةُ الْفَصْلِ

A Mamluk Qur'ān

A major feature observed in the Qur'āns of this chapter is that of illuminated opening pages, often called 'carpet' pages but more accurately known as 'incipit' or frontispiece pages. Their purpose is to awe readers and to immediately direct their attention to the glory of God and the divine glory of his book. This is an early example of a manuscript with decorated opening pages. This manuscript also possesses a colophon, a statement of when the manuscript was inscribed, in this case 1252/650. The scribe's name is not given, perhaps out of a concern that all of the glory should go to God. This Qur'ān was produced during the Mamluk dynasty. The script of the surah titles is given in a heavily lined, majestic *thuluth* script, and the text in a more delicately drawn and elegant *muhaqqaq* hand, two of the six scripts mentioned earlier.

MS. Huntington 37 fol. 2v, 3r; *Sūrat al-Fātihah* (The Opening), 1:1–7 and *Sūrat al-Baqarah* (The Cow), 2:1–4; 1252/650.

A luxury Mamluk edition

This manuscript was produced later in the Mamluk era and shows an increased use of gold and intricate technique in the illuminations. It is a spectacular manuscript, both for its rarity and for the visual impact of its artwork. The colophon in this manuscript gives the date, 1364/766, and the scribe, Umar bin Uthman Al Ja'fari Al Shafi'i. Pictured are the opening incipit pages orienting the reader to the greatness of God and his word. The script for the text is a fine *naskh*, and then for the surah titles it is an ornate homage to the new style which preceded the six scripts. The overall effect in gold and deep blue is a powerful one, conveying majesty, dignity, grace and power. The Mamluks reinstated the trend of producing large, beautiful Qur'āns, impressive in physical size and in their immediate visual impact.

MS. Canonici Or. 123 fol. 2v, 3r; *Sūrat al-Fātihah* (The Opening), 1:1–7 and *Sūrat al-Baqarah* (The Cow), 2:1–4; 1364/766.

THE MAJESTIC HEIGHTS OF QUR'ĀNIC ART

Books smile as pens shed tears.
al-'Attabi (d. 823/208 or 835/220)

THE QUR'ĀNS IN THIS CHAPTER REPRESENT THE PINNACLE OF Islam's art of the book. They bring together supreme artistic vision with exquisite workmanship and materials to serve what to Muslims is the most profound, sacred, mysterious and foundational theological truth—that the Holy Qur'ān is the manifestation of the Divine Presence in this material world. The Qur'āns pictured in this chapter span six centuries and many dynasties. Once the techniques involved in producing these magnificent books were perfected, basic styles and conventions of decoration spread throughout Turkish, Middle Eastern, Persian and Central Asian domains, and then succeeding and competing dynasties would rival each other to produce books of greater and more awe-inspiring beauty. The greatest empires in Islamic history expended considerable wealth and effort in their production. Examples in this chapter come from the Persian and Ottoman empires, the most prolific producers of luxury Qur'āns, as well as Central Asian Turkmen and Timurid Qur'āns.

The monetary amounts expended are incalculable, both figuratively and literally. Though the books speak for themselves in the supreme level of their quality, records have not come down to us as to how much they cost, nor how many man-hours were spent in their production, nor how many people were involved as scribes, illuminators and binders, though the industries to support such works of art were substantial and extensive.

Although the books command our attention, just behind the page are the scribes and illuminators, often anonymous or known to us only as a name in a colophon. Though supreme artists, in their piety they chose to have their Qur'āns stand in the limelight and receive the attention that in any other arena the artist would receive. And calligraphers did achieve fame as the supreme artists in the Muslim world with examples of their craft, whether for Qur'āns or for poetry, becoming collectible and scribes attracting the patronage of kings. The calligraphers were also closely associated with the mystical brotherhoods of the Sufis. In their personal striving for perfection and mystical union with the divine, they also sought to infuse their work with the same perfection. They filled the illuminations with sacred symbolism. Behind the intricate patterns of arabesques, vines, flowers and palmettes there are precise geometrical designs, arranged with internalized meanings of divine symbolism which they thought bridged the material and eternal spheres. By filling the opening pages of the Qur'āns with these works of art surrounding, reinforcing, supporting and focusing attention on the words of the sacred text, the scribes were seeking to lead readers out of the mundane physical world of daily care into the timeless, eternal realm of beauty and power in the eternal presence of God. Since these Qur'āns were so valuable, they came to be used not only as collectible items for kings and the wealthy, but also as diplomatic gifts, and even as objects of plunder in times of war.

A humble volume
in *muhaqqaq*

This is the final section of what was originally a thirty-volume Qur'ān comprising the last thirty-seven surahs. The last of thirty divisions of roughly equal length, it was used for personal and public recitation of the Qur'ān over a month. One belief celebrated in the fasting month of Ramadan is the revelation of the Qur'ān, and nightly in mosques around the world one of these thirty sections of the Qur'ān is recited publicly from memory. This manuscript is undated, but it came into the Bodleian's collection in the mid-1600s/1000s. Written in a bold and elegant script style called *muhaqqaq*, this style was popular between the twelfth/sixth and fifteenth/ninth centuries while continuing in lesser use for further centuries. This edition was also economical, written on inexpensive paper and with an undecorated but durable binding. The simple dignity of the elegant script maintains the aura of sacred majesty for the book.

MS. Seld. Sup. 64 fol. 4v, 5r; *Sūrat an-Naba'* (The Great News), 78:1–8; pre-1600/1000.

بِسۡمِ اللّٰهِ الرَّحۡمٰنِ الرَّحِيۡمِ

عَمَّ يَتَسَآءَلُوۡنَ عَنِ النَّبَإِ

الۡعَظِيۡمِ الَّذِىۡ هُمۡ فِيۡهِ

مُخۡتَلِفُوۡنَ كَلَّا سَيَعۡلَمُوۡنَ

ثُمَّ كَلَّا سَيَعۡلَمُوۡنَ اَلَمۡ

نَجۡعَلِ الۡاَرۡضَ مِهٰدًا وَّالۡجِبَالَ

اَوۡتَادًا وَّخَلَقۡنٰكُمۡ اَزۡوَاجًا

A *muhaqqaq* page with translation and hadith

Multi-volume Qur'āns with five or three lines of cursive script per page, such as this one, appear to have been produced in Anatolia, modern-day Turkey, in the decades following the conquest of Baghdad by the Mongols, which occurred in 1256/654. Yet the inclusion of a Persian translation, elegantly arranged in zigzag fashion underneath each verse, indicates that this copy was intended for a Persian-speaking user, suggesting a broader geographic attribution. Scholars have remarked on the archaic features exhibited by the monumental script used to copy this text—*muhaqqaq*—a fact that could reinforce an early date for this manuscript. At least one volume of the set, the one to which the present leaf originally belonged, appears to have been illuminated with an elaborate border of fine gold scrollwork featuring excerpts from the hadith (wise sayings attributed to the prophet Muhammad) that proclaim the virtues of reciting the Qur'ān.

EA2012.69 © Ashmolean Museum, University of Oxford. *Sūrat an-Nisa'* (the Women), 4:174; late 13th/7th–early 14th/8th century.

فوجد اموالهم وله

اَلنَّاسُ قَدْ جَاءَكُم

بُرْهَانٌ مِّن رَّبِّكُمْ

وَأَنزَلْنَا اِلَيْكُم نُورًا

An opulent edition

This extremely luxurious decorated Qur'ān is one of the finest featured in this book. On the pictured incipit pages there is a lavish use of gold and lapis lazuli, colours that speak not just of wealth and power of the patron, but of divine light and celestial glory. This lavish use of gold and lapis lazuli continues on every one of the following 602 pages. It is a large volume worthy of royalty and for proclaiming the exalted claims of the text. The text is written in a fine *muhaqqaq* script, with the titles in a flowing *thuluth* script. There are intricate braided borders, floral arabesques and intricate vinework detailing, which all combine to a harmonious and stunning visual effect, perhaps evoking in an abstract way the gardens of paradise. The manuscript, obtained in 1714/1126, has similar features to many fifteenth- and sixteenth-century Persian and Ottoman Qur'āns.

MS. Canonici Or. 121 fol. 2v, 3r; *Sūrat al-Fātihah* (The Opening), 1:1–7 and *Sūrat al-Baqarah* (The Cow), 2:1–4; 16th/10th century?

بسم الله الرحمن الرحيم
الحمد لله رب العالمين
الرحمن الرحيم
مالك يوم الدين اياك نعبد واياك
نستعين اهدنا الصراط المستقيم
صراط الذين انعمت عليهم
غير المغضوب عليهم ولا الضالين

بسم الله الرحمن الرحيم
الم ذلك الكتاب لا ريب فيه
هدى للمتقين الذين يؤمنون بالغيب
ويقيمون الصلوة ومما رزقناهم ينفقون
والذين يؤمنون بما انزل اليك وما انزل
من قبلك

A Safavid masterpiece

A rival to the last entry, this is a sixteenth/tenth-century Persian Safavid-dynasty Qur'ān. The pages pictured are the frontispiece pages, immediately preceding the text of the Qur'ān. The round medallions are called *shamsas* or 'suns'; they were often put in these luxury Qur'āns to awe the reader with the glory of God and his word. The Qur'ān texts inscribed on the tops and bottoms of the pages are verses from *Sūrat al-Wāqi'ah* 56:77–80 stressing the holiness and purity of the Qur'ān and the need for ritual purity when reading it. In the miniature suns, *Sūrat al-Isra'* 17:88 is spread between both, asserting that neither humanity nor spiritual beings could even together produce a book like the Qur'ān. Its remaining 598 pages are also decorated extensively in gold and lapis lazuli. This book was obtained in India in 1843/1259 and came to the Bodleian in a 1909/1327 bequest.

MS. Arab. d. 98 fol. 1v, 2r; *Sūrat al-Wāqi'ah* (The Event), 56:77–80 and *Sūrat al-Isrā'* (The Night Journey), 17:88; 16th/10th century; binding shown on p. 58.

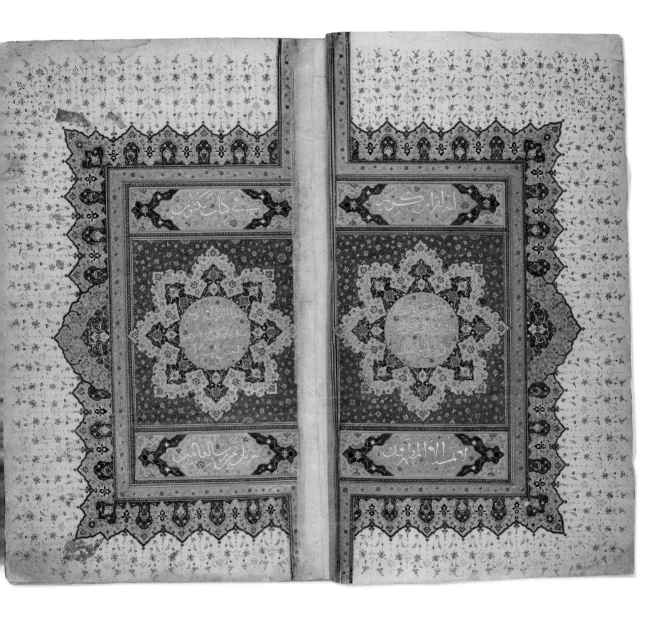

An ambassador's prize book

Manuscripts often combine beauty with an element of politics. This Qur'ān was the personal possession of Sir Gore Ouseley, British Ambassador to Persia from 1810/1225 until 1814/1229. As with the other luxury Qur'āns featured, one is struck by the stunning palette of colours on display, the interplay of floral arabesques with the carefully executed borders and braiding, the generous use of gold and the rich lapis lazuli blue, and the exquisite detail of design, craftsmanship and execution. Here the incipit pages present the opening chapters of the Qur'ān, the text in a flowing *naskh* script and the titles in stately *thuluth*. The script rests on cloud banks, which themselves rest on the divine light provided by the gold. The remaining 862 pages also have the script resting on gold clouds. These techniques all seek to enhance the divine credentials and experience of the text.

MS. Ouseley Add. 3 fol. 2v, 3r; *Sūrat al-Fātihah* (The Opening), 1:1–7 and *Sūrat al-Baqarah* (The Cow), 2:1–4; 1709/1121.

A Timurid jewel?

Yet another Qur'ān representing the height of Islam's art of the book, these decorated pages also present the opening chapters of the Qur'ān with the words resting on banks of clouds in the heavenly realms. The floral arabesques and the gem-like qualities of the tiny flowers suggest the gardens of paradise further above those realms. Again there is the lavish use of gold and blue, and rare among Qur'āns in this or any era is the use of pink for the opening surah titles. The Timurids of central Asia are said to have introduced the use of this colour into their Qur'āns, though this manuscript is possibly later than their era of the fifteenth/ninth century. Behind the intricate floral patterns there is a careful geometrical layout of sacred mystical symbolism reinforcing all the sacred associations of the text and the Qur'ān's exalted place in the cosmos.

MS. Bodl. Or. 95 fol. 4v, 5r; *Sūrat al-Fātihah* (The Opening), 1:1–7 and *Sūrat al-Baqarah* (The Cow), 2:1–4; 15th/9th–16th/10th century?

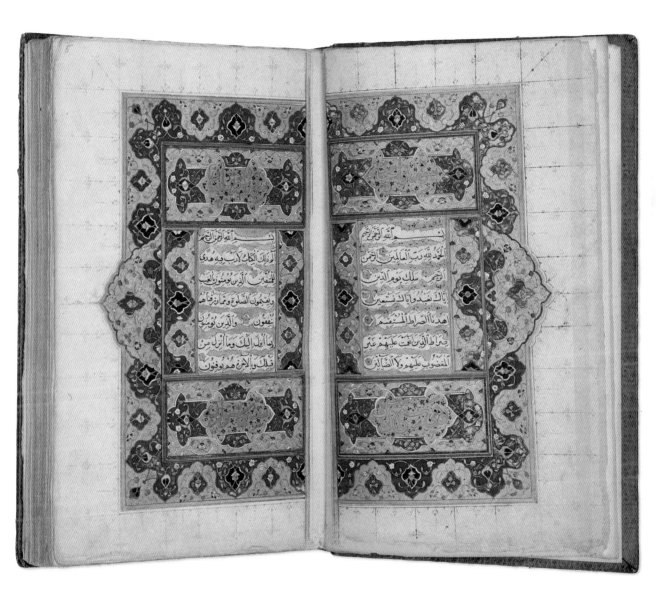

بسم الله الرحمن الرحيم
الحمد لله رب العالمين الرحمن
الرحيم ملك يوم الدين
اياك نعبد واياك نستعين
اهدنا الصراط المستقيم
صراط الذين انعمت عليهم غير
المغضوب عليهم ولا الضالين

بسم الله الرحمن الرحيم
الم ذلك الكتاب لا ريب فيه هدى
للمتقين الذين يؤمنون بالغيب
ويقيمون الصلوة ومما رزقناهم
ينفقون والذين يؤمنون
بما انزل اليك وما انزل من
قبلك وبالآخرة هم يوقنون

Beauty for moderate means

This manuscript of moderate quality and its interior pages use gold for text boxes and surah title boxes. While the use of gold is prolific, it is not as luxurious nor technically accomplished a production as other Qur'āns of this era; it reflects the market that beautiful Qur'āns were produced at various levels of affordability. It retains its original binding. The script style of the text is *naskh* and that of the titles is *thuluth*, a pattern common in Ottoman Qur'āns. This manuscript came into the Bodleian's collection in a 1640/1050 donation by Sir Kenelm Digby, who had attended the University of Oxford. He was a diplomat on behalf of King Charles I as well as an adventurer, a naval commander, a philosopher, an alchemist and a scientist. Many well-travelled men of this era learned Arabic for its practical uses in business, diplomacy and scholarship.

MS. Digby Or. 2 fol. 4v, 5r; *Sūrat al-Fātihah* (The Opening), 1:1–7 and *Sūrat al-Baqarah* (The Cow), 2:1–4; 17th/11th century.

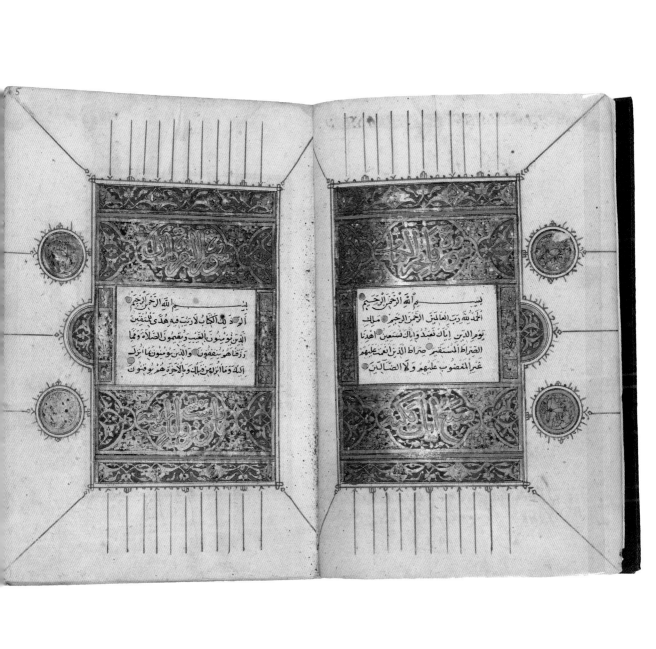

بسم الله الرحمن الرحيم
الحمد لله رب العالمين الرحمن الرحيم ملك
يوم الدين إياك نعبد وإياك نستعين اهدنا
الصراط المستقيم صراط الذين أنعمت عليهم
غير المغضوب عليهم ولا الضالين

بسم الله الرحمن الرحيم
الم ذلك الكتاب لا ريب فيه هدى للمتقين
الذين يؤمنون بالغيب ويقيمون الصلاة وما
رزقناهم ينفقون والذين يؤمنون بما أنزل
إليك وما أنزل من قبلك وبالآخرة هم يوقنون

An Ottoman pocket Qur'ān

Similar to eighteenth/twelfth century Ottoman Qur'āns, this Qur'ān has an architectural aspect to its decoration, which also includes a slightly different and more subdued colour palette than has been seen so far. Its effect, while beautiful, is less awe-inspiring and more approachable. The pavilion arch capping the surah title text boxes is supported by columns filled with braided bands. The banded boxes are used to organize the page, and the floral arabesques almost disappear behind the architectural elements. The text, in *naski* script, is resting on clouds with golden divine light peeking out between them from behind. *Thuluth* script again is used for the titles. Throughout the Qur'ān the text is contained within gold frames with gold surah title boxes containing multicoloured highlights. The paper quality, together with the technical accomplishment of the illuminations exhibits qualities of moderate production values. It is bound in its original binding.

MS. Ind. Inst. Arab. 24 fol. ɪv, 2r; *Sūrat al-Fātiḥah* (The Opening), 1:1–7 and *Sūrat al-Baqarah* (The Cow), 2:1–5; 18th/12th century?

An Ottoman
compact Qur'ān

This manuscript, with its Ottoman-style floral features, has simpler,
more naturalistic yet still abstract, flowers and greenery instead of
highly stylized arabesques. The colours are vivid and yet subdued,
giving an overall effect that is more contemplative and restful than
humbling or awe-inspiring. It continues the long-standing convention
of *naskh* text resting on cloud scrolls, but the clouds are regularized
and the gold margins which provide the outlines of the clouds have
straight edges. The text of the initial two surahs is inscribed in two
circular panels framed by braided boxes—an uncommon convention
in Qur'āns from this era. Gold text frames are used throughout
the entire book as well as gold surah title boxes. The book has an
1872/1289 donation date in its cover and its binding is similar to other
nineteenth/thirteenth century Ottoman Qur'āns. It also exhibits a
moderate quality of production in its paper and illuminations.

MS. Ind. Inst. Arab. 21 fol. 1v, 2r; *Sūrat al-Fātihah* (The Opening), 1:1–7 and *Sūrat al-Baqarah*
(The Cow), 2:1–5; 19th/13th century; p. ii shows the binding.

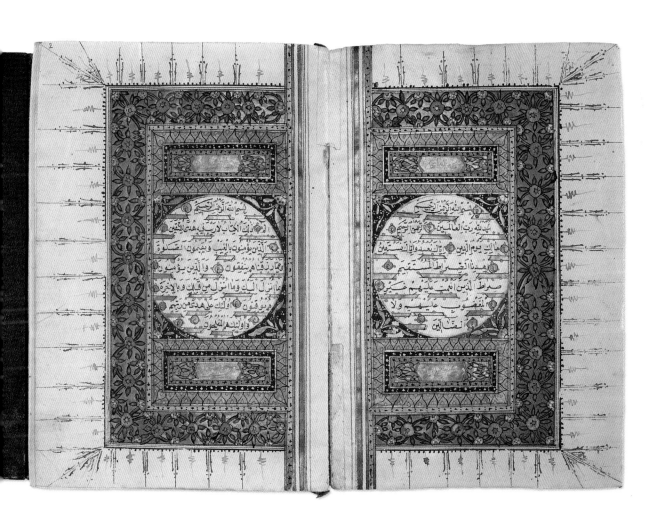

A Qajar masterpiece

A luxury pocket Qur'ān of the highest quality, this manuscript is from the Qajar era in nineteenth/thirteenth-century Iran. On these incipit pages, every available space is filled with deep, rich colour and intricate floral arabesques. There are also precise chained borders framing the opening texts of the first two surahs. Throughout the book, the text is framed in gold and every surah has its title framed in a gold box with floral arabesques. At the end of the book are pages devoted to Arabic script divination rubrics, a common feature in many Persian Qur'āns of this and earlier eras. The overall effect conveys a majesty far outweighing the modest size of the volume. This Qur'ān is also signed by the scribe, one Muhammad Hashim al-Isfahani, who finished it on a Thursday, the 18th day in the Islamic month of Sha'bān—the year and location are not given.

MS. Arab. g. 27 fol. 2v, 3r; *Sūrat al-Fātiḥah* (The Opening), 1:1–7 and *Sūrat al-Baqarah* (The Cow), 2:1–4; 19th/13th century.

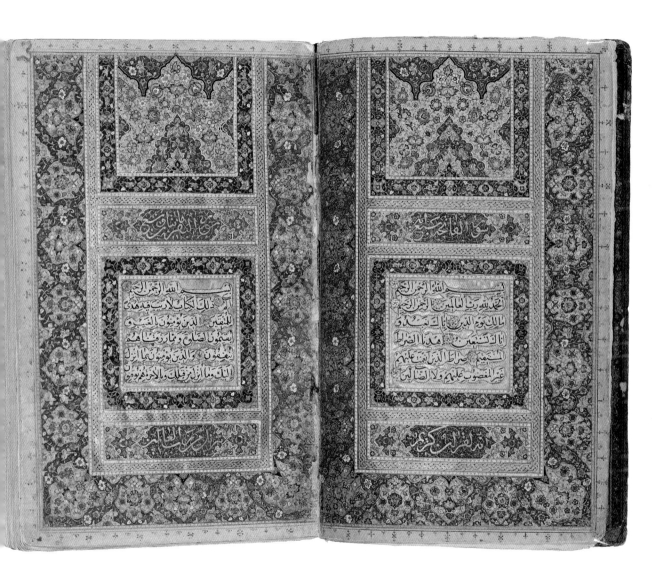

A refurbished Turkmen leaf

This fine folio comes from a sumptuous Qur'ān made for Ya'qub Beg (r. 1478/883–1490/895), the leader of the Aq Qoyunlu, a Turkmen dynasty which controlled Eastern Turkey, Iraq and Iran until 1508/914. The page was originally at the beginning of part sixteen of a thirty-volume Qur'ān, as suggested by the illuminated frame (*sarlawh*) surrounding its verses, a feature traditionally used in Islamic manuscripts to mark the start of a new section. The inscriptions in the two cartouches located on the upper margin further confirm this. These two bands were originally placed side by side across a double-page opening, but ended up on the same page, compromising its original symmetry, as a result of a later attempt to refurbish the folio. However, the use of multiple scripts per page inscribed in bands of varying widths and heights is genuine and was increasingly adopted in Qur'āns produced from the fifteenth/ninth century onwards.

EA2012.71, © Ashmolean Museum, University of Oxford. *Sūrat al-Kahf* (The Cave), 18:77–80; 1483/888.

هذا الجزء السادس عشر

مجمله أجزاء القرآن الثلاثين

عَلَيْهِ أَجْرًا ۞ قَالَ هَذَا فِرَاقُ بَيْنِي وَبَيْنِكَ سَأُنَبِّئُكَ بِتَأْوِيلِ مَا لَمْ تَسْتَطِع عَّلَيْهِ صَبْرًا ۞ أَمَّا السَّفِينَةُ فَكَانَتْ لِمَسَاكِينَ

يَعْمَلُونَ فِي الْبَحْرِ فَأَرَدتُّ أَنْ أَعِيبَهَا وَكَانَ

وَرَاءَهُم مَّلِكٌ يَأْخُذُ كُلَّ سَفِينَةٍ غَصْبًا ۞ وَأَمَّا الْغُلَامُ فَكَانَ أَبَوَاهُ مُؤْمِنَيْنِ فَخَشِينَا أَن يُرْهِقَهُمَا طُغْيَانًا وَكُفْرًا

تَنزِيلٌ مِّن رَّبِّ الْعَالَمِينَ

EUROPEAN RENAISSANCE ENCOUNTERS WITH THE QUR'ĀN

Sum Thomæ Erpenÿ
Ex dono Clarissimi
viri
Isaaci Casauboni.
anno 1610

From the sublime to the prosaic, the Qur'āns of this chapter provide a contrast to preceding ones, in that they are ordinary books with sturdy bindings meant to be studied and used rather than admired for their beauty. These Qur'āns were used by scholars in Renaissance Europe for technical academic work. During this era Arabic became a university subject in the major centres of Europe, and Qur'āns were especially sought out by scholars because of their usefulness for learning Arabic and also for understanding Islamic religion, theology, law and culture.

When the Bodleian Library was founded in 1602/1010, Europe was experiencing a period of economic and political expansion which brought increased contact and conflict with Muslims as trade routes opened to the Far East. There was a growing desire for knowledge of all aspects of Islam, including its practices, history, politics and scholarship. In the rush for knowledge, one source at hand was the Arabic books coming onto the market from plunder in piracy and war. Other books and manuscripts were obtained in the less dramatic but more reliable fashion of scholars travelling to cities like Istanbul, Aleppo, Damascus and Cairo seeking out and purchasing them for themselves and their universities. These scholars were discovering a new world of Islamic scholarship that had developed over centuries and was largely unknown to the West.

In some ways, this European scholarship represents a final flowering of medieval scholarship concerning Islam, but now equipped with a fresh mindset that sought to understand Islam through its own sources and on its own terms. Chief centres of study were Oxford, Cambridge, Heidelberg, Leiden, Vienna and Breslau. Some notable scholars were the Englishmen William Bedwell, Edward Pococke and Thomas Adams, the Dutch linguist Thomas Erpenius, the French Huguenot scholar Isaac Casaubon, and the German scholar Jacob Christmann. They were starting to explore the centuries-old world of Islamic scholarship, which focused on consolidating and continuing their traditional scholarly disciplines. However, the Western scholars were also asking questions that were not being pursued in Islamic circles. Their questions and approaches were moulded by the Enlightenment and the Protestant Reformation— approaches that strongly challenged deeply entrenched traditional views. For the Qur'ān, it meant looking to establish its text from contemporary and ancient manuscripts, rather than just accepting a traditional form of the text. This was what was being done in manuscript studies of the New Testament and the Hebrew Bible. For example, the Dutch scholar Desiderius Erasmus in the 1500s/900s had been producing various critical editions of the Greek New Testament based on newly discovered and analysed ancient New Testament manuscripts. Scholars just after Erasmus' era attempted similar projects for the Qur'ān but in the end their work was not continued and is only now being pursued as thoroughly as they intended.

A Latin Qur'ān translation

This twelfth/sixth century Latin paraphrase of the Qur'ān by Robert of Ketton, a medieval theologian from Lincolnshire, is found in a thirteenth/seventh-century compendium of works concerning Islam. In the wake of the Crusades, volumes like this were produced to help Europeans in their growing contacts with Muslims, though the tone of many of the works was polemical and dismissive. Robert of Ketton's version of the Qur'ān was one of the earliest translations into a Western language, and it became the most used version of the Qur'ān in Europe until the seventeenth/eleventh century. Though there are some mistakes in his translation, his work is an honourable one, marked by a sincere and non-polemical approach to capture the sense of the Qur'ān as Muslims would have wanted it understood. To do this, he not only learned Arabic; he also consulted standard Muslim commentaries on the Qur'ān.

MS. Seld. Sup. 31 fol. 32v and 33r; *Sūrat al-Fātiḥah* (The Opening), 1:1–7 and *Sūrat al-Baqarah* (The Cow), 2:1–14; 13th/7th century.

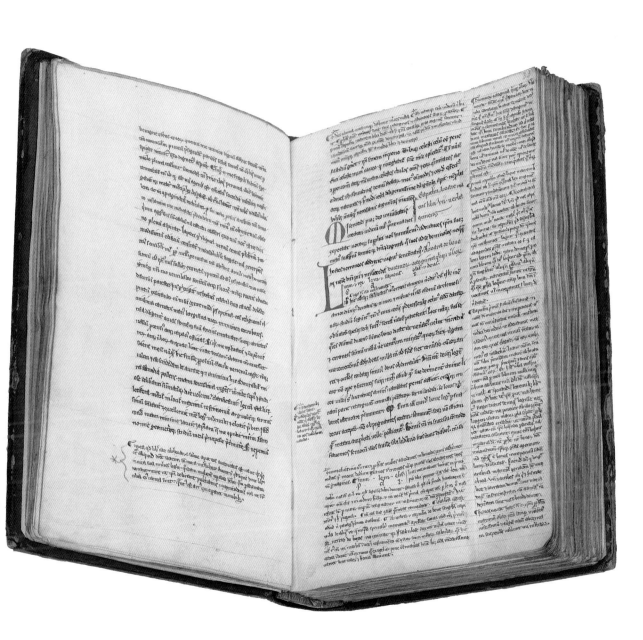

A Qur'ān for academic study

A humble edition of the Qur'ān, this book was produced without expensive illuminations, with a sturdy binding and a clear, readable text. Instead of using a double-page illuminated frontispiece with the first surah being given its own special treatment, the text simply starts at the top of the first page and continues from there. It is a Qur'ān for reading and practical use rather than for show. This Qur'ān was presented to Thomas Bodley by John Wrothe in 1601/1009 and was present in the Bodleian's collection as its first Arabic manuscript when the library opened in 1602/1010. At that time, this volume was almost new, its colophon mentioning its date of inscription as 1584/992. The scribe's name is not mentioned. The text is written in a clear *naskh* script and the surah titles are in red *thuluth* script, as are the symbols marking the ends of verses.

MS. Bodl. Or. 322 fol. 1v, 2r; *Sūrat al-Fātiḥah* (The Opening), 1:1–7 and *Sūrat al-Baqarah* (The Cow), 2:1–23; 1584/992.

سورة فاتحة الكتاب أيا مكية

بسم الله الرحمن الرحيم

الحمد لله رب العالمين الرحمن الرحيم مالك يوم الدين إياك
نعبد وإياك نستعين اهدنا الصراط المستقيم صراط الذين
أنعمت عليهم غير المغضوب عليهم ولا الضالين

سورة البقرة مدنية

بسم الله الرحمن الرحيم

الم ذلك الكتاب لا ريب فيه هدى للمتقين الذين
يؤمنون بالغيب ويقيمون الصلاة ومما رزقناهم ينفقون
والذين يؤمنون بما أنزل إليك وما أنزل من قبلك وبالآخرة
هم يوقنون أولئك على هدى من ربهم وأولئك هم المفلحون
إن الذين كفروا سواء عليهم أأنذرتهم أم لم تنذرهم لا يؤمنون
ختم الله على قلوبهم وعلى سمعهم وعلى أبصارهم غشاوة ولهم
عذاب عظيم ومن الناس من يقول آمنا بالله وباليوم الآخر وما هم
بمؤمنين يخادعون الله والذين آمنوا وما يخدعون إلا
أنفسهم وما يشعرون في قلوبهم مرض فزادهم الله مرضا
ولهم عذاب أليم بما كانوا يكذبون وإذا قيل لهم

لا تفسدوا في الأرض قالوا إنما نحن مصلحون ألا إنهم هم المفسدون
ولكن لا يشعرون وإذا قيل لهم آمنوا كما آمن الناس قالوا أنؤمن كما
آمن السفهاء ألا إنهم هم السفهاء ولكن لا يعلمون وإذا لقوا الذين
آمنوا قالوا آمنا وإذا خلوا إلى شياطينهم قالوا إنا معكم إنما
نحن مستهزئون الله يستهزئ بهم ويمدهم في طغيانهم يعمهون أولئك الذين
اشتروا الضلالة بالهدى فما ربحت تجارتهم وما كانوا
مهتدين مثلهم كمثل الذي استوقد نارا فلما أضاءت ما
حوله ذهب الله بنورهم وتركهم في ظلمات لا يبصرون
صم بكم عمي فهم لا يرجعون أو كصيب من السماء فيه ظلمات ورعد
وبرق يجعلون أصابعهم في آذانهم من الصواعق حذر الموت
والله محيط بالكافرين يكاد البرق يخطف أبصارهم
كلما أضاء لهم مشوا فيه وإذا أظلم عليهم قاموا ولو شاء الله لذهب
بسمعهم وأبصارهم إن الله على كل شيء قدير يا أيها الناس
اعبدوا ربكم الذي خلقكم والذين من قبلكم لعلكم تتقون
الذي جعل لكم الأرض فراشا والسماء بناء وأنزل من السماء ماء
فأخرج به من الثمرات رزقا لكم فلا تجعلوا لله أندادا وأنتم
تعلمون وإن كنتم في ريب مما نزلنا على عبدنا فأتوا بسورة

William Bedwell's personal notebook

This small notebook contains the personal notes of William Bedwell (1561/968–1632/1041), an accomplished scholar in Semitic languages who is held by many to be responsible for the revival of scholarly interest in Arabic in 1600s/1000s Europe. Bedwell, who taught himself Arabic through translating Arabic manuscripts of the early Christian Fathers, taught many European scholars their Arabic, including Oxford's first chair of Arabic studies, Edward Pococke. He was a man of wide-ranging interests. King James I appointed him to one of the committees responsible for translating from Hebrew the first twelve Old Testament books for the Authorized Version of the Bible. In this small notebook a few portions of the Qur'ān are transcribed, as well as some explanations of the names of a few stars. Arabic was required by scholars in the European renaissance for reading the Arabic works in astronomy, mathematics and medicine, as well as for religious works.

MS. Laud Or. 319 fol. 1v, 2r; *Sūrat an-Naba'* (The Great News), 78:1–14; 17th/11th century.

بِسْمِ اللَّهِ الرَّحْمَٰنِ الرَّحِيمِ
عَمَّ يَتَسَاءَلُونَ عَنِ النَّبَإِ
الْعَظِيمِ الَّذِي هُمْ فِيهِ
مُخْتَلِفُونَ كَلَّا سَيَعْلَمُونَ
ثُمَّ كَلَّا سَيَعْلَمُونَ أَلَمْ نَجْعَلِ
الْأَرْضَ مِهَادًا وَالْجِبَالَ

أَوْتَادًا وَخَلَقْنَاكُمْ أَزْوَاجًا
وَجَعَلْنَا نَوْمَكُمْ سُبَاتًا
وَجَعَلْنَا اللَّيْلَ لِبَاسًا
وَجَعَلْنَا النَّهَارَ مَعَاشًا
وَبَنَيْنَا فَوْقَكُمْ سَبْعًا
شِدَادًا وَجَعَلْنَا سِرَاجًا
وَهَّاجًا وَأَنْزَلْنَا مِنَ

A geometry professor's notebook

A pocket exercise book, this notebook was owned and made by John Greaves, a geometry professor who became the Savillian Professor of Astronomy at Oxford. A compendium showing an interest in matters well outside his scientific disciplines, it contains excerpts from Islamic history books and various chapters of the Qur'ān. Pictured are the pages which present the beginning of *Sūrat al-Kahf*, chapter 18, 'The Cave'. This chapter contains the Qur'ān's version of the story known from earlier Christian Syriac sources as The Seven Sleepers of Ephesus. In this notebook, Greaves transcribed and then translated the Qur'ān's text into Latin, the scholarly language of the day, in the space between the lines of Arabic text. Greaves travelled widely and collected manuscripts for the Bodleian's collection for Chancellor and Archbishop William Laud. During the English Civil War, in 1649/1059, Greaves was ejected from his Oxford professorship because of his royalist sympathies.

MS. Greaves 32 fol. 5v, 6r; *Sūrat al-Kahf* (The Cave), 18:1–11; 17th/11th century.

سورة الكهف

18.

بسم الله الرحمن الرحيم

الحمد لله الذي انزل على عبده الكتاب

ولم يجعل له عوجا قيما لينذر بأسا

شديدا من لدنه ويبشر المؤمنين الذين

يعملون الصالحات ان لهم اجرا حسنا

ماكثين فيه ابدا وينذر الذين قالوا

اتخذ الله ولدا ما لهم به من علم

ولا لآبائهم كبرت كلمة

تخرج من افواههم ان يقولون

فلعلك باخع نفسك على

ان لم يؤمنوا بهذا الحديث

انا جعلنا ما على الارض زينة

لها لنبلوهم ايهم احسن عملا

وانا لجاعلون ما عليها صعيدا

ام حسبت ان اصحاب الكهف والرقيم كانوا من آياتنا عجبا

اذ اوى الفتية الى الكهف فقالوا ربنا آتنا من لدنك رحمة

وهيئ لنا من امرنا رشدا فضربنا

على آذانهم في الكهف سنين عددا

A reverend's notebook

In this personal exercise book, a reverend and fellow of the Royal Society, Richard Rawlinson, transcribed and then translated into Latin an important section of the Qur'ān for Christians and Muslims. This section exhibits relationships to the biblical Gospel's account of Jesus' birth and identity as well as views from later Christian literature concerning Jesus. *Sūrat Maryam* (Mary), chapter 19, recounts the Islamic version of the story of the miraculous conception of Jesus. It also has one of the Qur'ān's main miracle stories in which Jesus—'Isa, by his Qur'ānic name—speaks while an infant from the cradle, defending his mother's honour while also asserting his identity as a human prophet in a way that denies Christian assertions of deity. Being one of the main points of difference and discussion between Christians and Muslims, this represents one clergyman's attempt to understand the Islamic view of Jesus on its own terms.

MS. Rawlinson Or. 2 fol. 22v, 23r; *Sūrat Maryam*, 19:1–22; 18th/12th century.

بسم الله الرحمن الرحيم ۞ كهيعص ۞ ذكر رحمة ربك عبده زكريا ۞ اذ نادى ربه نداء خفيا ۞ قال رب اني وهن العظم مني واشتعل الراس شيبا ولم اكن بدعائك رب شقيا ۞ واني خفت الموالي من ورائي وكانت امراتي عاقرا فهب لي من لدنك وليا ۞ يرثني ويرث من ال يعقوب واجعله رب رضيا ۞ يا زكريا انا نبشرك بغلام اسمه يحيى لم نجعل له من قبل سميا ۞ قال رب انى يكون لي غلام وكانت امراتي عاقرا وقد بلغت من الكبر عتيا ۞ قال كذلك قال ربك هو علي هين وقد خلقتك من قبل ولم تك شيئا ۞ قال رب اجعل لي آية قال آيتك الا تكلم الناس ثلاث ليال سويا ۞ فخرج على قومه من المحراب

فاوحى اليهم ان سبحوه بكرة وعشيا ۞ يا يحيى خذ الكتاب بقوة واتيناه الحكم صبيا ۞ وحنانا من لدنا وزكوة وكان تقيا ۞ وبرا بوالديه ولم يكن جبارا عصيا ۞ وسلام عليه يوم ولد ويوم يموت ويوم يبعث حيا ۞ واذكر في الكتاب مريم اذ انتبذت من اهلها مكانا شرقيا ۞ فاتخذت من دونهم حجابا فارسلنا اليها روحنا فتمثل لها بشرا سويا ۞ قالت اني اعوذ بالرحمن منك ان كنت تقيا ۞ قال انما انا رسول ربك لاهب لك غلاما زكيا ۞ قالت انى يكون لي غلام ولم يمسسني بشر ولم اك بغيا ۞ قال كذلك قال ربك هو علي هين ولنجعله آية للناس ورحمة منا وكان امرا مقضيا ۞ فحملته فانتبذت به مكانا

A German scholar's Qur'ān

This Qur'ān is an example of the wider European scholarly interest in Arabic, having come from the collection of a German scholar, Jacob Christmann, Professor of Arabic at Heidelberg, Germany. Christmann was appointed to the second professorial chair in Arabic in Europe in 1609/1018. Paris established the first one in 1535/941. Chancellor and Archbishop William Laud established Oxford's chair in 1636/1045. This Qur'ān came into the possession of the chaplain to the British envoy in Germany, Samson Johnson, in 1635/1044; he passed it to Chancellor Laud. This Qur'ān is a sturdy production, more for personal use than for show. Its script is written in a clear, flowing *naskh* script with surah titles in red. This era produced a remarkable band of European scholars who collaborated to produce scholarship of Arabic and Islamic cultures based on accurate understanding of Arabic sources, instead of continuing the polemical lines of medieval literature.

MS. Laud Or. 246 fol. 1v, 2r; *Sūrat al-Fātiḥah* (The Opening), 1:1–7 and *Sūrat al-Baqarah* (The Cow), 2:1–5; 16th/10th century.

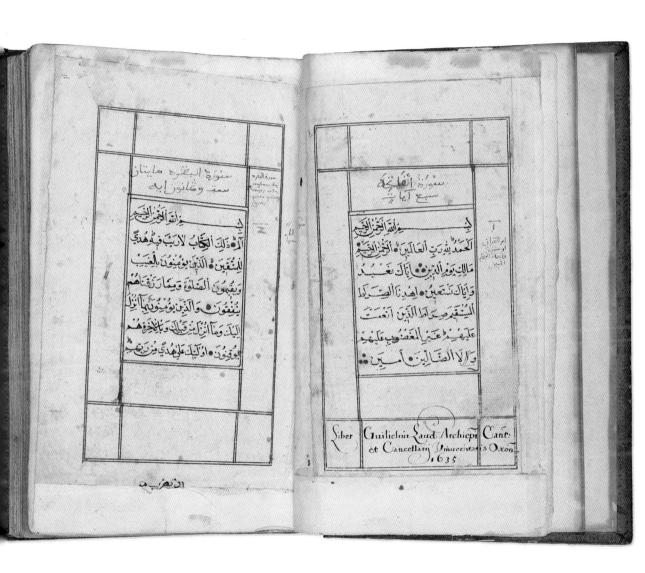

سورة الفاتحة
سبع آيات

بسم الله الرحمن الرحيم
الحمد لله رب العالمين الرحمن الرحيم
مالك يوم الدين اياك نعبد
واياك نستعين اهدنا الصراط
المستقيم صراط الذين انعمت
عليهم غير المغضوب عليهم
ولا الضالين آمين

سورة البقرة مائتان
وسبع وثمانون آية

بسم الله الرحمن الرحيم
الم ذلك الكتاب لا ريب فيه هدى
للمتقين الذين يؤمنون بالغيب
ويقيمون الصلاة ومما رزقناهم
ينفقون والذين يؤمنون بما انزل
اليك وما انزل من قبلك وبالآخرة هم
يوقنون اولئك على هدى من ربهم

A Qur'ān with scholars' notes

This Qur'ān passed through the hands of six European Arabic scholars.
Two of them were especially famous in their day: Thomas Erpenius, Professor
of Arabic at the University of Leiden, known throughout Europe for his
command of oriental languages, and Isaac Casaubon, held to be the most
learned man in Europe at that time. Casaubon gave this Qur'ān to Erpenius
in 1610/1019, three years before Casaubon settled in Oxford and only four
years before what many considered a premature death. His scholarly fame led
to his burial in Westminster Abbey near Poets' Corner. This Qur'ān is special
in another way—it has marginal notes recording textual variants attributed
to four prominent early Qur'ān reciters. These notations, made by a Dutch
Arabist Adriaen Willemsz, and added to by Erpenius, reflect the value then
being placed on recovering the earliest forms of ancient scriptural texts, like
the Old and New Testaments.

MS. Marsh 358 fol. 305v; *Sūrat al-Humazah* (The Slanderer), 104:1 through to *Sūrat al-Māʿūn*
(The Small Kindnesses), 107:5; 16th/10th century; pp. 86–7 show fol. 307v.

(9)

306

Ibn Amir, Hamza, Kisai, BRd.
cum Rasched d. maijoribus literis scriptum est al. 1.1.

ali. BRd.

BRd.
Kisai

Cuth. Supplem.
BRd.

ali. BRd.

ويل لكل همزة لمزة ۝ الذي جمع مالا وعدده يحسب ان
ماله اخلده ۝ كلا لينبذن في الحطمة ۝ وما ادرك ما الحطمة ۝
نار الله الموقدة ۝ التي تطلع على الافئدة ۝ انها عليهم مؤصدة ۝
في عمد ممددة ۝ سورة الفيل مكية وايها خمس آيات

بسم الله الرحمن الرحيم

الم تر كيف فعل ربك باصحاب الفيل ۝ الم يجعل كيدهم في تضليل ۝
وارسل عليهم طيرا ابابيل ۝ ترميهم بحجارة من سجيل ۝
فجعلهم كعصف مأكول ۝ سورة قريش مكية وفيها اربع آيات

بسم الله الرحمن الرحيم

لايلاف قريش ۝ الافهم رحلة الشتاء والصيف ۝ فليعبدوا
رب هذا البيت ۝ الذي اطعمهم من جوع وامنهم من خوف ۝
سورة الماعون مكية وايها سبع آيات

بسم الله الرحمن الرحيم

ارايت الذي يكذب بالدين ۝ فذلك الذي يدع اليتيم ۝ ولا يحض
على طعام المسكين ۝ فويل للمصلين ۝ الذين هم عن صلاتهم

A critical text of the Qur'ān?

This partial Qur'ān is perhaps a unique achievement for its time, and a significant one since. It is a Qur'ān that combines the readings of three manuscripts into one text. This is similar to texts being produced for the New Testament of the Bible in Greek in the 1500s/900s and 1600s/1000s, which were being used as the basis for vernacular translations in Europe. Establishing as sound a base text as possible, scholars were collating manuscripts to evaluate variations that might be later changes to the text. These scholarly editions are known as critical texts. This Qur'ān in concept is a critical text, containing a marginal apparatus to highlight textual variants. This one collates three manuscripts, one apparently from the Middle East, one from Africa, and one from Asia. It was produced by William Guise, an Arabic and Hebrew scholar and Fellow of All Souls College.

MS. Marsh 533 fol. 45r; *Sūrat At-Taubah* (The Repentance), 9:54–70; 17th/11th century.

الله فيجحدوا ما حرم الله الذين امنوا لهم من اعمالهم والله لا يهدي القوم الكفرين ۝ يا ايها الذين امنوا ما لكم اذا قيل لكم انفروا في سبيل الله اثاقلتم الى الارض ارضيتم بالحيوة الدنيا من الاخرة فما متاع الحيوة الدنيا في الاخرة الا قليل ۝ الا تنفروا يعذبكم عذابا اليما ويستبدل قوما غيركم ولا تضروه شيا والله على كل شي قدير ۝ الا تنصروه فقد نصره الله اذ اخرجه الذين كفروا ثاني اثنين اذ هما في الغار اذ يقول لصاحبه لا تحزن ان الله معنا فانزل الله سكينته عليه وايده بجنود لم تروها وجعل كلمة الذين كفروا السفلى وكلمة الله هي العليا والله عزيز حكيم ۝ انفروا خفافا وثقالا وجاهدوا باموالكم وانفسكم في سبيل الله ذلكم خير لكم ان كنتم تعلمون ۝ لو كان عرضا قريبا وسفرا قاصدا لاتبعوك ولكن بعدت عليهم الشقة وسيحلفون بالله لو استطعنا لخرجنا معكم يهلكون انفسهم والله يعلم انهم لكاذبون ۝ عفا الله عنك لم اذنت لهم حتى يتبين لك الذين صدقوا وتعلم الكاذبين ۝ لا يستأذنك الذين يؤمنون بالله واليوم الاخر ان يجاهدوا باموالهم وانفسهم والله عليم بالمتقين ۝ انما يستأذنك الذين لا يؤمنون بالله واليوم الاخر وارتابت قلوبهم فهم في ريبهم يترددون ۝ ولو ارادوا الخروج لاعدوا له عدة ولكن كره الله انبعاثهم فثبطهم وقيل اقعدوا مع القاعدين ۝ لو خرجوا فيكم ما زادوكم الا خبالا ولاوضعوا خلالكم يبغونكم الفتنة وفيكم سماعون لهم والله عليم بالظالمين ۝ لقد ابتغوا الفتنة من قبل وقلبوا لك الامور حتى جا الحق وظهر امر الله وهم كارهون ۝ ومنهم من يقول ائذن لي ولا تفتني الا في الفتنة سقطوا وان جهنم لمحيطة بالكافرين ۝ ان تصبك حسنة تسؤهم وان تصبك مصيبة يقولوا قد اخذنا امرنا من قبل ويتولوا وهم فرحون ۝ قل لن يصيبنا الا ما كتب الله لنا هو مولانا وعلى الله فليتوكل المؤمنون ۝ قل هل تربصون بنا الا احدى الحسنيين ونحن نتربص بكم ان يصيبكم الله بعذاب من عنده او بايدينا فتربصوا انا معكم متربصون ۝ قل انفقوا طوعا او كرها لن يتقبل منكم انكم كنتم قوما فاسقين ۝ وما منعهم ان تقبل منهم

نفقاتهم الا انهم كفروا بالله ورسوله ولا ياتون الصلوة الا وهم كسالى ولا ينفقون الا وهم كارهون ۝ فلا تعجبك اموالهم ولا اولادهم انما يريد الله ليعذبهم بها في الحيوة الدنيا وتزهق انفسهم وهم كافرون ۝ ويحلفون بالله انهم لمنكم وما هم منكم ولكنهم قوم يفرقون ۝ لو يجدون ملجا او مغارات او مدخلا لولوا اليه وهم يجمحون ۝ ومنهم من يلمزك في الصدقات فان اعطوا منها رضوا وان لم يعطوا منها اذا هم يسخطون ۝ ولو انهم رضوا ما اتاهم الله ورسوله وقالوا حسبنا الله سيؤتينا الله من فضله ورسوله انا الى الله راغبون ۝ انما الصدقات للفقراء والمساكين والعاملين عليها والمؤلفة قلوبهم وفي الرقاب والغارمين وفي سبيل الله وابن السبيل فريضة من الله والله عليم حكيم ۝ ومنهم الذين يؤذون النبي ويقولون هو اذن قل اذن خير لكم يؤمن بالله ويؤمن للمؤمنين ورحمة للذين امنوا منكم والذين يؤذون رسول الله لهم عذاب اليم ۝ يحلفون بالله لكم ليرضوكم والله ورسوله احق ان يرضوه ان كانوا مؤمنين ۝ الم يعلموا انه من يحادد الله ورسوله فان له نار جهنم خالدا فيها ذلك الخزي العظيم ۝ يحذر المنافقون ان تنزل عليهم سورة تنبئهم بما في قلوبهم قل استهزءوا ان الله مخرج ما تحذرون ۝ ولئن سالتهم ليقولن انما كنا نخوض ونلعب قل ابالله وايته ورسوله كنتم تستهزءون ۝ لا تعتذروا قد كفرتم بعد ايمانكم ان نعف عن طائفة منكم نعذب طائفة بانهم كانوا مجرمين ۝ المنافقون والمنافقات بعضهم من بعض يامرون بالمنكر وينهون عن المعروف ويقبضون ايديهم نسوا الله فنسيهم ان المنافقين هم الفاسقون ۝ وعد الله المنافقين والمنافقات والكفار نار جهنم خالدين فيها هي حسبهم ولعنهم الله ولهم عذاب مقيم ۝ كالذين من قبلكم كانوا اشد منكم قوة واكثر اموالا واولادا فاستمتعوا بخلاقهم فاستمتعتم بخلاقكم كما استمتع الذين من قبلكم بخلاقهم وخضتم كالذي خاضوا اولئك حبطت اعمالهم في الدنيا والاخرة واولئك هم الخاسرون ۝ الم ياتهم نبا الذين من قبلهم قوم نوح وعاد وثمود

بِسْمِ اللّٰهِ الرَّحْمٰنِ الرَّحِيمِ

الْحَمْدُ لِلّٰهِ رَبِّ الْعَالَمِينَ ۞ الرَّحْمٰنِ الرَّحِيمِ ۞ مَالِكِ

يَوْمِ الدِّينِ ۞ إِيَّاكَ نَعْبُدُ وَإِيَّاكَ نَسْتَعِينُ ۞

اهْدِنَا الصِّرَاطَ الْمُسْتَقِيمَ ۞ صِرَاطَ

الَّذِينَ أَنْعَمْتَ عَلَيْهِمْ غَيْرِ الْمَغْضُوبِ

عَلَيْهِمْ ۞ وَلَا الضَّالِّينَ

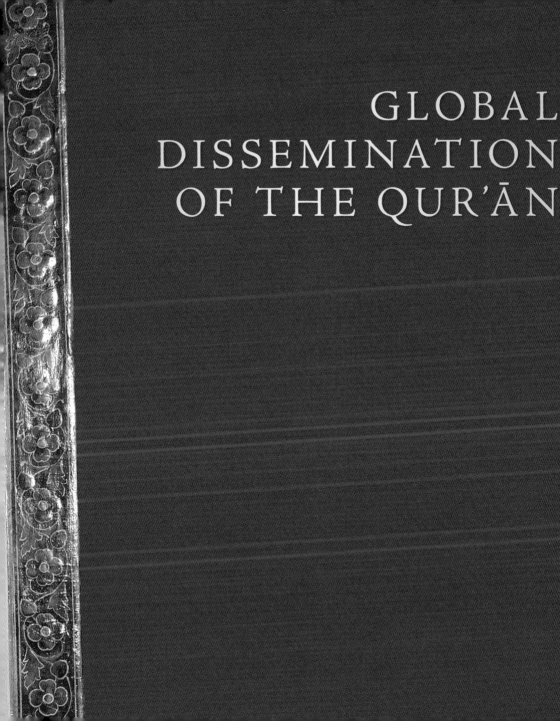

GLOBAL
DISSEMINATION
OF THE QUR'ĀN

I N THE FOURTEEN CENTURIES OF ITS EXISTENCE IN WRITTEN FORM, the Qur'ān has spread to every continent, including Antarctica. Wherever Muslims have lived, it has been read and recited, and in most places transcribed and printed. Historically, most Qur'āns have been produced in North and West Africa, the Middle East, Central Asia, Persia and India—the traditional Muslim heartlands. During the centuries of Islam's territorial expansion and entry into global trade, Qur'āns have spread throughout the world and have come to exist in a wide variety of book forms and artistic styles. European collections, like the Bodleian's, contain representative samples obtained from many different continents. These manuscripts were obtained as purchases, but also as bequests and gifts from merchants, soldiers, adventurers, scholars, diplomats, clerics and nobility.

The global stylistic diversity of the artwork is striking, as also are the differences in the quality of production and the technical requirements applied in the construction of book bindings to meet different local conditions. The spectrum of these approaches is pictured in this chapter. There are luxurious

Qur'āns commissioned by royal and wealthy patrons from Persia and the Ottoman Empire. In striking contrast is a more humble African loose-leaf affair kept together and carried in a rough but sturdy untanned leather case.

Also, one encounters slightly different versions of the text of the Qur'ān in the form of precise historical recitations recorded in writing. Especially in the African Qur'āns one finds four slightly different versions of the Qur'ān, all of which are found in print today, known by the names of the early reciters from whom they are held to be passed down. These four are the recitations of Abu Bakr 'Asim (d. 745/127) via Hafs ibn Sulayman (d. 796/180), Nafi' al-Madani (d. 785/168) via 'Uthman ibn Sa'id Warsh (d. 813/197), Abu 'Amr ibn 'Ala' (d. *ca.* 770/153) though Hafs al-Duri (d. 860/246). (One can also find on the Internet recordings of modern Qur'ān reciters speaking these versions.)

Taken together, these Qur'ān manuscripts provide an important resource for historical research documenting the use of the Qur'ān in various eras and geographical localities, documenting how the Qur'ān has been used in various versions, and tracing its textual development through the centuries. They also provide windows on significant political dramas where books can become powerful symbols in geopolitical events. MS. Bodl. Or. 793 is one such symbol, a luxurious edition which was a twice-plundered pawn in the political fortunes of two monarchs—Tipu Sultan, the 'Tiger of Mysore', and King George III.

Another, showing the depth and breadth of ordinary piety, is the well-used personal Qur'ān MS. Arab. d. 140, obtained from a religious teacher in the Northwest Frontier area of Pakistan, before the partition of British India into the independent countries of India, Pakistan and Bangladesh.

A devotional section from North Africa

This manuscript is the fourth volume from what was originally a sixty-volume Qur'ān. Each volume contained one *hizb*, one sixtieth, of the Qur'ān. A *hizb* is half a *juz*, a division read during the nights of Ramadan and also for personal devotions. This *hizb* contains surah 2:203–253. Historically, Qur'āns have often been bound in multi-volume sets of various sizes—five, thirty or sixty volumes, for instance—and were often kept in special boxes or pieces of furniture made to house them. The title on the page shown is not for a surah but for the beginning of this particular *hizb*. The form of the text is distinctive to north-west Africa, a version named after a prominent early Egyptian Qur'ān reciter 'Uthman ibn Sa'id Warsh (d. 813/197). Its text is written in *maghribi* script, a style also distinctive to north-west Africa, with its titles in *thuluth* script.

MS. Laud Or. 72 fol. 5r, 6v; *Sūrat al-Baqarah* (the Cow), 2:203–206; 16th/10th–17th/11th century.

واذكروا الله في أيام
معدودت فمن تعجل
في يومين فلا اثم عليه
ومن تأخر فلا اثم عليه
لمن اتقى واتقوا الله
واعلموا انكم اليه
تحشرون ومن الناس

من يعجبك قوله في الحيو
الدنيا ويشهد الله على
ما في قلبه وهو الد
الخصام واذا تولى سعى
في الارض ليفسد فيها
ويهلك الحرث والنسل
والله لا يحب الفساد
واذا قيل له اتق الله
اخذته العزة بالاثم

A Mauritanian Qur'ān portion

This Qur'ān portion was obtained from Mauritania, perhaps originally through trade contacts. It was originally from a multi-volume Qur'ān, and this page shows the beginning of a *hizb* section (one sixtieth of the Qur'ān) that starts with *Sūrat ar-Rahmān*, 'The Merciful', surah number 55. This volume contains just this surah, though the full *hizb* continues through the next two surahs. This volume also contains some added material—instructions for how properly to perform the purification washings before prayer, and also a sermon from a sheikh. It was rebound at some point after coming into Western hands. This was acquired during the period of the great seventeenth/eleventh-century manuscript acquisitions in the West, when European scholars and politicians were taking an increased interest in North and West Africa. The Barbary states and Mauritania were influential Islamic regional powers and European libraries were working to gather information on the religion, culture and history of the region.

MS. Bodl. Or. 478 fol. 1v, 2r; *Sūrat ar-Rahmān* (The Merciful), 55:1–27; 16th/10th–17th/11th century.

سورة الرحمن مكية

بِسْمِ اللَّهِ الرَّحْمَٰنِ الرَّحِيمِ
الرَّحْمَٰنُ عَلَّمَ الْقُرْآنَ خَلَقَ الْإِنْسَانَ
عَلَّمَهُ الْبَيَانَ الشَّمْسُ وَالْقَمَرُ
بِحُسْبَانٍ وَالنَّجْمُ وَالشَّجَرُ يَسْجُدَانِ
وَالسَّمَاءَ رَفَعَهَا وَوَضَعَ الْمِيزَانَ
أَلَّا تَطْغَوْا فِي الْمِيزَانِ وَأَقِيمُوا
الْوَزْنَ بِالْقِسْطِ وَلَا تُخْسِرُوا
الْمِيزَانَ وَالْأَرْضَ وَضَعَهَا
لِلْأَنَامِ فِيهَا فَاكِهَةٌ وَالنَّخْلُ
ذَاتُ الْأَكْمَامِ وَالْحَبُّ ذُو الْعَصْفِ

وَالرَّيْحَانُ فَبِأَيِّ آلَاءِ رَبِّكُمَا
تُكَذِّبَانِ خَلَقَ الْإِنْسَانَ مِنْ
صَلْصَالٍ كَالْفَخَّارِ وَخَلَقَ الْجَانَّ
مِنْ مَارِجٍ مِنْ نَارٍ فَبِأَيِّ آلَاءِ رَبِّكُمَا
تُكَذِّبَانِ رَبُّ الْمَشْرِقَيْنِ وَرَبُّ
الْمَغْرِبَيْنِ فَبِأَيِّ آلَاءِ رَبِّكُمَا تُكَذِّبَانِ مَرَجَ الْبَحْرَيْنِ يَلْتَقِيَانِ بَيْنَهُمَا
بَرْزَخٌ لَا يَبْغِيَانِ فَبِأَيِّ آلَاءِ رَبِّكُمَا
تُكَذِّبَانِ يَخْرُجُ مِنْهُمَا اللُّؤْلُؤُ
وَالْمَرْجَانُ فَبِأَيِّ آلَاءِ رَبِّكُمَا تُكَذِّبَانِ
وَلَهُ الْجَوَارِ الْمُنْشَآتُ فِي الْبَحْرِ
كَالْأَعْلَامِ فَبِأَيِّ آلَاءِ رَبِّكُمَا
تُكَذِّبَانِ كُلُّ مَنْ عَلَيْهَا فَانٍ
وَيَبْقَىٰ وَجْهُ رَبِّكَ ذُو الْجَلَالِ وَالْإِكْرَامِ

An exuberant Qur'ān from Ghana

This partial Qur'ān demonstrates the tremendous variety one encounters with Qur'āns from Africa. This one is from what is now Ghana, and is notable for its lively artwork, uncommon in its vivacity and exuberance. This artwork, together with the carefully executed *maghribi* script and the multicoloured pointing, marks this out as a production of particularly high quality. Folio 19 has a particularly ornate surah title for *Sūrat Maryam*, number 19, noting the beginning of the second half of the Qur'ān. Folio 112 contains a playful decorative marginal designation for a *hizb* section. This Qur'ān was brought out from the interior of Africa by a native chief and given to a British major-general, Luke Smythe O'Connor, in the 1850s/1270s. O'Connor was the commander of British forces headquartered at Cape Coast Castle, formerly a notorious slave-trade depot. This Qur'ān is thought to have been inscribed in the 1840s/1260s.

MS. Arab. e. 101 fol. 19, 112; *Sūrat Maryam* (Mary), 19:1–2 and *Sūrat Yā Sīn*, 36:25–33; 19th/13th century.

الا نتبع جوا وقالوا ارثنا بما يعلم انا اليكم
مرسلون قمووما علينا الا البلغ المبين
قالوا انا تطيرنا بكم لين لم تنتهوا لنرجمنكم
جمنكم وليمسنكم منا عذاب اليم له
قالوا طيركم معكم اين ذكرتم بل انتم
قوم مسرفون وجا من اقصا المدينة
رجل يسعى قال يقوم اتبعوا المرسلين
اتبعوا من لا يسئلكم اجرا وهم مهتدون
وما لي لا اعبد الذي فطرني واليه ترجعون
اانخذ من دونه الهة ان يردن الرحمن
بضر لا تغن عني شفعتهم شيا
ولا ينقذون اني اذا لفي ضلل مبين

ابي ... امنت برنكم فاشمعون ... فيل
ادخل الجنة قال يليت قومي يعلمون
بما غفر لي ربي وجعلني من المكرمين
وما انزلنا على قومه من بعده من جند
من السما وما كنا منزلين ان كانت
الا صيحة واحدة فاذا هم خمدون
يحسرة على العباد ما ياتيهم من رسول
الا كانوا به يستهزون الم يروا كم
اهلكنا قبلهم من القرون انهم اليهم
لا يرجعون وان كل لما جميع لدينا
محضرون له واية لهم الارض الميتة
احييناها واخرجنا منها حبا فمنه ياكلون

An East African unbound Qur'ān

This Qur'ān is typical of East Africa in that it is unbound, its pages
stacked in order and kept together in a simple, untreated leather pouch.
It has very simple artwork and presents the text with an inelegant and
untidy but mainly serviceable *naskh* script that is typical for its era
and region. It is a Qur'ān for daily personal use and was a well-used
and valued possession. It was found at Omdurman, Sudan in 1943/1363
and possibly dates back to the 1800s/1200s. Its text has interesting
composite features. Its script uses spelling conventions like those used
in the Eastern Islamic domains rather than Western ones. However,
its pronunciation for recitation is more in line with that further west in
North Africa, that of the famous Qur'ān reciter Warsh, and it also has
features of another early reciter whose version was used in Sudan, that of
al-Duri from Abu 'Amr.

MS. Arab. d. 215 fol. 1r; *Sūrat al-Baqarah* (The Cow), 2:1–5; 19th/13th century?

A Turkish translation

The Qur'ān has been translated into and printed in more than sixty-five languages, and we can lose appreciation of the relative newness of access to the Qur'ān in vernacular languages. Interlinear handwritten manuscript translations of the Qur'ān are relatively rare, and ones in Turkish or Persian are the most prevalent historically. This one was written in the Islamic month Muharram 978 or 25 June 1570 by Mehmed ibn Mustafa, known by the pen name Bulka'i. In 1948/1367, the Bodleian Library purchased this Qur'ān from Oskar Rescher, a German–Turkish Orientalist scholar. Rescher had served the German government and academic establishment in various capacities during World War I and after. He settled in Istanbul, continuing his studies, representing the German academic establishment and collecting manuscripts. In 1933/1352, while he was living in Istanbul, the Nazis revoked his permission to lecture in German universities. In 1937/1356 he took Turkish citizenship.

MS. Turk. e. 75 fol. 1v, 2r; *Sūrat al-Fātiḥah* (The Opening), 1:1–7 and *Sūrat al-Baqarah* (The Cow), 2:1–4; 16th/10th century.

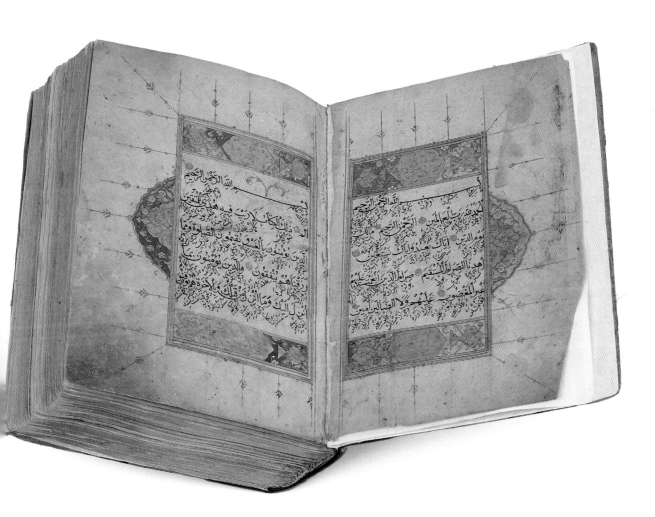

An illuminated Qur'ān

This manuscript is either a Persian or an Ottoman Qur'ān of medium quality, from an era when the Persian and Ottoman empires were artistic rivals as well as political ones. At first they shared many decorative conventions; later they started to develop distinguishable styles. Both regions were producing Qur'āns of intricate design, using floral arabesques, *naskh* script and vibrant colours to draw the reader in with light, grace and beauty. It is thought that this manuscript was among a group of manuscripts given to the Bodleian after the death of Professor Thomas Hunt, Laudian Professor of Arabic from 1738/1151–1774/1188. After his death parcels of manuscripts and books were found in his study in Christ Church, but it is a mystery as to how they were obtained. They were perhaps gifts to the library that had been 'intercepted' by Hunt before they had been catalogued and put into the collection properly.

MS. Bodl. Or. 136 fol. 1v, 2r; *Sūrat al-Fātiḥah* (The Opening), 1:1–7 and *Sūrat al-Baqarah* (The Cow), 2:1–4; 18th/12th century?

A Persian Safavid masterpiece

This Safavid Persian Qur'ān represents the summit of Islamic book art, and the climax of the artistic embodiment of the theology of the Qur'ān, with its luxuriant colours and intricate and extensive craftsmanship. Its history also combines elements of religious devotion and political intrigue. It was commissioned as a pious act by a wealthy patron, yet it was plundered more than two hundred years later by the Indian ruler Tipu Sultan of Mysore. When he was defeated in 1799/1214 by Colonel Arthur Wellesley, Tipu's own library was taken as spoil by the British East India Company. This Qur'ān was given to Oxford University by the directors of the East India Company in 1806/1221, and other Qur'āns from Tipu Sultan's library were given as gifts to Cambridge University, St Andrews University and the Crown. Wellesley went on to become the Duke of Wellington, who defeated Napoleon at Waterloo in 1813/1228.

MS. Bodl. Or. 793 fol. 9v, 10r; *Sūrat al-Fātiḥah* (The Opening), 1:1–7; 1550/957.

A Persian Qajar masterpiece

This is a Persian Qajar-era Qur'ān, continuing and developing the Safavid tradition into the 1800s/1200s, using rich, deep colours with jewel-like emphases. *Naskh* script is used for the text and is written on cloud scrolls. Floral arabesques surround the text in well-organized boxes. The surah titles are written in the stately *thuluth* script. This Qur'ān also has military connections—but to more recent turbulent political events. It was donated to the Bodleian in 1992/1412 by General Fereydoun Jam, a retired four-star general who had served the Shah of Iran for decades as supreme commander of the armed forces and as ambassador to Spain; at one point he was married to one of the Shah's sisters. In early 1979/1400, after refusing to take a post in the reform government of Shahpour Bakhtiar, General Jam retired to London immediately before the Iranian Revolution that brought the Ayatollah Khomeini to power.

MS. Arab. b. 13 fol. 3v, 4r; *Sūrat al-Fātiḥah* (The Opening), 1:1–7 and *Sūrat al-Baqarah* (The Cow), 2:1–4; 19th/13th century.

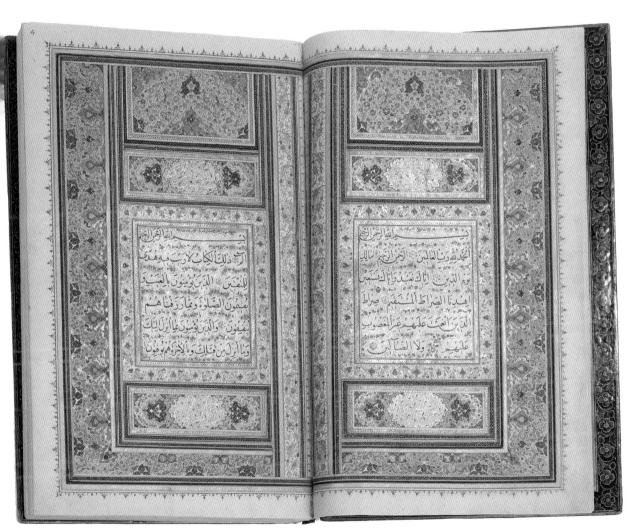

An Indian Qur'ān

This page originates from a large codex attributable to India. Its thirteen lines per page are written in a local script known as *bihari*, a cursive style whose origins are still debated but which was specific to religious texts in the pre-Mughal period. The use of black and red ink—here employed for the first, intermediate and last line on each page—adds rhythm to the text block, reflecting a practice frequently seen in the Indian production of this period. Red is also used for the interlinear Persian translation in *naskh* placed underneath each verse, while the word *Allah* is singled out and highlighted in gold. The Persian translation is duplicated on the margin and is often accompanied by a more extensive commentary on each passage. Five more folios from the same manuscript (*Sūrat Yūsuf*, 12:92–*Sūrat al-Raʿd*, 13:31) are also in the Ashmolean collection.

EA1990.1271 © Ashmolean Museum, University of Oxford. *Sūrat al-Raʿd* (The Thunder), 13:6–12; 15th/9th–16th/10th century.

المثلات وان ربك لذو مغفرة للناس على
ظلمهم وان ربك لشديد العقاب ويقول
الذين كفروا لولا انزل عليه ءاية من ربه انما
انت منذر ولكل قوم هاد ۞ الله يعلم ما تحمل
كل انثى وما تغيض الارحام وما تزداد و
كل شيء عنده بمقدار ۞ عالم الغيب والشهادة
الكبير المتعال ۞ سواء منكم من اسر القول
ومن جهر به ومن هو مستخف بالليل وسارب
بالنهار له معقبات من بين يديه ومن
خلفه يحفظونه من امر الله ان الله لا يغير ما
بقوم حتى يغيروا ما بانفسهم واذا اراد الله
بقوم سوءا فلا مرد له وما لهم من دونه من
وال ۞ هو الذي يريكم البرق خوفا وطمعا و

A Northwest Frontier Qur'ān

This is the well-used personal Qur'ān of a Muslim leader who lived in what is now the Northwest Frontier province of Pakistan. From all indications, it was a treasured possession—possibly a family heirloom— which had seen a useful life over perhaps a couple of centuries. Its pages are worn, damaged and carefully repaired. There are many annotations and some corrections in the text. It is a production of low artistic quality yet with a sturdy binding and a clear text written in black *naskh* script with red surah titles. The incipit pages follow a very simple decorative plan, with the pages laid out in boxes made up of fine lines of red for the text with the surah titles also in red ink. The remaining pages are laid out within simple red-lined text boxes as well. It is still in its original binding.

MS. Arab. d. 140 fol. 1v, 2r; *Sūrat al-Fātiḥah* (The Opening), 1:1–7 and *Sūrat al-Baqarah* (The Cow), 2:1–4; 18th/12th–19th/13th century?

PERSONAL MANUSCRIPTS OF THE QUR'ĀN

The Mansab came this morning, and brought a very precious possession, a manuscript copied by his grandfather ... a sort of commonplace book of all that was thought worth preserving at that time. It has the fascination of old and treasured things, gathered for someone's private joy.

Freya Stark

THE PREVIOUS CHAPTERS HAVE TRACED THE DEVELOPMENT OF the Qur'ān, from its humble beginnings to the exquisite and unsurpassed pinnacles reached in the Islamic art of the book. This has followed the geographical spread of the Qur'ān through much of the world, as well as opening a small window on the history of European encounters with the Qur'ān—and Oxford University's significant role in the dissemination of knowledge of Arabic and Islam in the European Renaissance. The Qur'āns featured on the following pages were originally produced for personal devotional use. These are the Qur'āns that ordinary people used to obtain the daily measure of comfort and assurance that the Divine One was personally interested in their affairs in the midst of the chaos and uncertainty of life. They were old and treasured things, passed down in families.

The theology attached to the Qur'ān leads it to being viewed as a powerful physical object in whatever form the words are inscribed. This has led to many ways in which the text of the Qur'ān is inscribed, either partially or in its entirety for use in amulets and talismans. This chapter contains a variety of these kinds of Qur'ān. Though their forms are diverse, they have several things in common. They are all intended to be worn on the person—under, in or on the clothing. They are also viewed as providing a protective effect by their mere presence. With their presence, though, they are all also intended to be read and prayed for their protective and curative effects to be fully realized. Also, these Qur'āns are great equalizers. Though a wealthy patron may expend considerable money commissioning a luxurious illuminated devotional collection like the one featured, MS. Arab. e. 182, since Allah is blind to distinctions of class and wealth, the prayers made from using a humble book like MS. Laud Or. 15 would be heard on the basis of the piety and sincerity of the individual, not the quality of their prayer book.

A personal devotional collection

This is an exceptionally fine eighteenth/twelfth century devotional book. It contains a personal selection of prayers and devotional material by famous religious teachers, selections from the Qur'ān and divination material, all carefully transcribed, illuminated and bound together within a quality Ottoman binding. It fits snugly in a tooled leather satchel, which originally came with a shoulder strap. The satchel is decorated with silver wire which spells out a verse from the Qur'ān, *Sūrat al-Wāqi'ah*, 56:79: 'None can touch it but the purified.' This verse has been interpreted variously as a warning to those who might use the book without due caution, as a signal that only the pure in heart can attain to the Qur'ān's deeper meanings, or that angels are the only ones able to touch the heavenly Qur'ān. The satchel was made later for the book and is dated 1889/1306. The book and its satchel were gifts to the Bodleian by twin brothers and collectors R.H. and T.G. Gayer-Anderson in 1943/1362.

MS. Arab. e. 182; Satchel (p. 139) and book; *Sūrat al-Wāqi'ah* (The Event), 56:79; 18th/12th and 19th/13th century.

Rare depictions of holy places

A special feature of this devotional book is that it contains dated illustrations of Islamic holy sites, having been completed in 1733/1146. These illustrations are of the sacred precincts of Medina and the tombs of Muhammad and two of his closest followers, Abu Bakr and 'Umar. These men were also two of his closest friends, two of his earliest converts, and the first two caliphs in succession after Muhammad's death in 632/11. Illustrations of these sites in Medina and also ones in Mecca can be found in devotional books like this from the eighteenth and nineteenth centuries. Historical illustrations in manuscripts like these are taking on new importance. Changes have been made to the holy sites to accommodate the vast numbers of pilgrims who visit Mecca and Medina, which has led to sacrificing some of the historic layout to ensure safety and access.

MS. Arab. e. 182 fol. 50v, 51r; illustration of Tombs of Muhammad and two caliphs; 18th/12th century.

A section of special prayers

The quality of illuminations in this book is of a level seen in Persian and Ottoman luxury Qur'āns, with the use of floral arabesques and gold as well as the careful techniques used for page layouts and dividing the book into sections with appropriate illuminations. This section is devoted to prayers written by famous religious scholars. These are ones which were composed in Mecca by a scholar named 'Ali b. Sultan Muhammad al-Qari' al-Harawi, who died in 1605/1013. He made a point of composing his prayers from sound traditions (*hadith*) in the Islamic literature. They were transcribed in 1733/1146. Some of the other scholars whose prayers feature in this small volume include a famous scholar, Muhammad al Ghazali at-Tusi (d. 1111/504), and a famous Qur'ān reciter, Muhammad b. al-Jazari (d. 1430/833). There is also a well-known medieval devotional book included by Abu 'Abdallah Muhammad b. Sulaiman al-Jazuli (d. 1465/869).

MS. Arab. e. 182 fol. 76v, 77r; Illuminations at the start of a section of prayers.

Special Qur'ān selections

At the end of the volume is the most sacred material—selections from the Qur'ān. Parts of three surahs are transcribed and illuminated along with other material with the care reserved for the finest ornamented Qur'āns. The portions used are from surahs 36, 48 and 17 and are often found in talismanic excerpts of the Qur'ān. They are thought to have a special power for protecting the possessor from harm—whether illness, injury or misfortune. Taken together, the elements of this volume not only combine to make this a book with comforting meaning derived from the supporting content of its diverse elements—it would also have been regarded as a supernaturally powerful object in itself. The book would have offered continued prayer for its wearer for protection from adversity. These features would have all combined to make it a greatly treasured possession for pious Muslims for many generations.

MS. Arab. e. 182 fol. 116r; *Sūrat Yā Sīn*, 36:1–12; 18th/12th century.

يٰس وَالْقُرْآنِ الْحَكِيمِ اِنَّكَ لَمِنَ الْمُرْسَلِينَ عَلٰى صِرَاطٍ مُسْتَقِيمٍ

تَنْزِيلَ الْعَزِيزِ الرَّحِيمِ لِتُنْذِرَ قَوْمًا مَا اُنْذِرَ اٰبَاؤُهُمْ

فَهُمْ غَافِلُونَ لَقَدْ حَقَّ الْقَوْلُ عَلٰى اَكْثَرِهِمْ فَهُمْ لَا يُؤْمِنُونَ

اِنَّا جَعَلْنَا فِي اَعْنَاقِهِمْ اَغْلَالًا فَهِيَ اِلَى الْاَذْقَانِ فَهُمْ مُقْمَحُونَ

وَجَعَلْنَا مِنْ بَيْنِ اَيْدِيهِمْ سَدًّا وَمِنْ خَلْفِهِمْ سَدًّا فَاَغْشَيْنَاهُمْ

فَهُمْ لَا يُبْصِرُونَ وَسَوَاءٌ عَلَيْهِمْ ءَاَنْذَرْتَهُمْ اَمْ لَمْ تُنْذِرْهُمْ

لَا يُؤْمِنُونَ اِنَّمَا تُنْذِرُ مَنِ اتَّبَعَ الذِّكْرَ وَخَشِيَ الرَّحْمٰنَ

بِالْغَيْبِ فَبَشِّرْهُ بِمَغْفِرَةٍ وَاَجْرٍ كَرِيمٍ اِنَّا نَحْنُ نُحْيِ الْمَوْتٰى

وَنَكْتُبُ مَا قَدَّمُوا وَاٰثَارَهُمْ وَكُلَّ شَيْءٍ اَحْصَيْنَاهُ فِي

اِمَامٍ مُبِينٍ اَللّٰهُمَّ سَخِّرْ لِي قُلُوبَ عِبَادِكَ كَمَا سَخَّرْتَ

فِرْعَوْنَ لِمُوسٰى وَلَيِّنْ لِي قُلُوبَ عِبَادِكَ كَمَا اَلَنْتَ الْحَدِيدَ

لِدَاوُدَ فَاِنَّهُمْ لَا يَنْطِقُونَ اِلَّا بِاِذْنِكَ نَوَاصِيهِمْ فِي قَبْضَتِكَ

وَقُلُوبُهُمْ فِي يَدِكَ جَلَّ ثَنَاؤُكَ يَا اَرْحَمَ الرَّاحِمِينَ

اَللّٰهُمَّ اجْذِبْ لِي رُوحَهُمْ وَجَسَدَهُمْ وَجَمِيعَ اَعْضَائِهِمْ

وَبِحَقِّ حَقِّكَ وَبِحَقِّ اَنْبِيَائِكَ وَالْمُرْسَلِينَ وَالنَّبِيِّينَ وَالْمَلَائِكَةِ

الْمُقَرَّبِينَ وَبِحَقِّ يٰس وَالْقُرْآنِ الْحَكِيمِ وَبِحَقِّ ذٰلِكَ

الْكِتَابُ لَا رَيْبَ فِيهِ هُدًى لِلْمُتَّقِينَ وَبِحَقِّ الٓمٓ اللهُ لَا اِلٰهَ

اِلَّا هُوَ الْحَيُّ الْقَيُّومُ وَبِحَقِّ الٓمٓصٓ وَبِحَقِّ الٓمٓرٰ كٓهٰيٰعٓصٓ وَطٰهٰ

وَحٰمٓ عٓسٓقٓ وَحٰمٓ وَالْكِتَابِ الْمُبِينِ وَبِحَقِّ صٓ وَالْقُرْآنِ ذِي الذِّكْرِ

وَبِحَقِّ قٓ وَالْقُرْآنِ الْمَجِيدِ وَبِحَقِّ وَالطُّورِ وَكِتَابٍ مَسْطُورٍ

فِي رَقٍّ مَنْشُورٍ وَالْبَيْتِ الْمَعْمُورِ وَالسَّقْفِ الْمَرْفُوعِ وَالْبَحْرِ

الْمَسْجُورِ وَبِحَقِّ نٓ وَالْقَلَمِ وَمَا يَسْطُرُونَ وَبِحَقِّ جَمِيعِ

سُوَرِ الْقُرْآنِ وَاضْرِبْ لَهُمْ مَثَلًا اَصْحَابَ الْقَرْيَةِ

A talismanic Qur'ān scroll

The text of the Qur'ān was used for protection from life's dangers in many ways. This solid gold case was used to carry the complete Qur'ān written on a scroll rolled up carefully and concealed within. The case would be fastened to the clothing with the red silk cord. The value of the case and especially the power of the words within were held to protect the person wearing the talisman from all manner of harm—whether physical danger, illness, misfortune or even crime. Talisman cases such as this were made of precious metals of all types, and were often intricately engraved and highly decorated with gems. This is a rare example of one that is completely devoid of decoration or engraving, yet it is still stunning in its simple beauty. One traveller to Egypt in the 1800s/1200s observed that such talismans were particularly popular with women.

MS. Arab. g. 5; Qur'ān scroll and gold case; 1814/1229.

A Qur'ān scroll
in a winding case

This is another example of a Qur'ān written on a scroll and kept within a case to be carried on the person. This case, though, is made from a dense, richly hued tropical hardwood turned carefully on a lathe. It also serves as a simple rewinding mechanism for the scroll. This scroll has the text of the Qur'ān beautifully inscribed in black and red, with green and gold decorations. The 'Throne Verse' *Sūrat al-Baqarah* 2:256, divided into eleven phrases, provides a coordinating organizational motif for the entire scroll, together with the script arranged in red flower shapes. This verse is held to contain particular power and majesty. Some of the text has been carefully worked into the shape of flowers, carefully written in the miniaturists' form of *naskh* called *ghubar* script. The scroll is similar in script and style to seventeenth/eleventh century Ottoman talismanic Qur'āns.

MS. Arab. g. 14; Qur'ān scroll and wooden case; 17th/11th century.

Miniature Qur'ān book

Miniature Qur'āns take many shapes. This one is in the form of a normal book, only of a minuscule size. It comes complete with a normal binding of tooled leather, decorated with gold and filigree. The opening pages are illuminated, like the much larger luxury Qur'āns, with floral motifs and the rich use of gold and deep blues. The text is then scaled down in perfect proportion to the page, the first surah on the right-hand page and the beginning of the second surah on the left-hand page. The script style is the miniaturists' script called *ghubar*. This Qur'ān would have been carried on the person as a protective talisman. Miniature Qur'āns were thought to be particularly powerful in their protective effects. As the physical embodiment of the eternal word of God, they were thought to be potentially the most powerful force a person could possess.

MS. Arab. g. 33 fol. 2v, 3r; Miniature Qur'ān book; *Sūrat al-Fātihah* (The Opening), 1:1–7 and *Sūrat al-Baqarah* (The Cow), 2:1–4; 17th/11th–19th/13th century; p. 134 shows the binding.

Octagonal miniature Qur'ān

This miniature demonstrates the creativity with which these books could be produced. The page size of this octagonal Qur'ān is the size of the face of a modern wristwatch, with sixteen lines of text on a page. With its ivory case, this would have been worn or carried in a person's clothing. The main function of this type of Qur'ān was as a talisman for supernatural protection. In ordinary circumstances it was protection from illness or misfortune. There are records of similar miniatures being hung from Ottoman battle standards for protection in time of war. These uses emphasize the deep belief and long history of the Qur'ān being viewed in itself as a book of divine presence and power. Octagonal miniature Qur'āns have been produced in Persian and Ottoman domains of the seventeenth/eleventh to nineteenth/thirteenth centuries. This miniature was owned by Bishop Narcissus Marsh, whose manuscript collection was given to the Bodleian in 1714/1126.

MS. Marsh 715; Octagonal Miniature Qur'ān and Ivory case; *Sūrat al-Fātiḥah* (The Opening), 1:1–7; 17th/11th century.

Qur'ān talismanic shirt

One of the most unusual forms the Qur'ān has taken in its history is one not of paper or parchment, but of textile. This is the text of the Qur'ān inscribed on a shirt to be worn for protection. Such shirts are rare in museum collections and become available on the antiquities market very infrequently. This shirt has survived in a very delicate condition and is similar to seventeenth/eleventh-century examples from northern India. These shirts were worn underneath armour when going into battle. In addition to verses from the Qur'ān, they can contain invocations for gaining courage or victory, solutions to problems, healing from injuries, strength in argument, defeating the Evil Eye, and many other problems associated with battle. Around the neck opening of this shirt and down the front are found some of the ninety-nine names of Allah—such as 'The Protector', 'The All-seeing', 'The All-knowing' and 'The All-forgiving'.

MS. Bodl. Or. 162; Qur'ān *jama* (shirt); 16th/10th century?

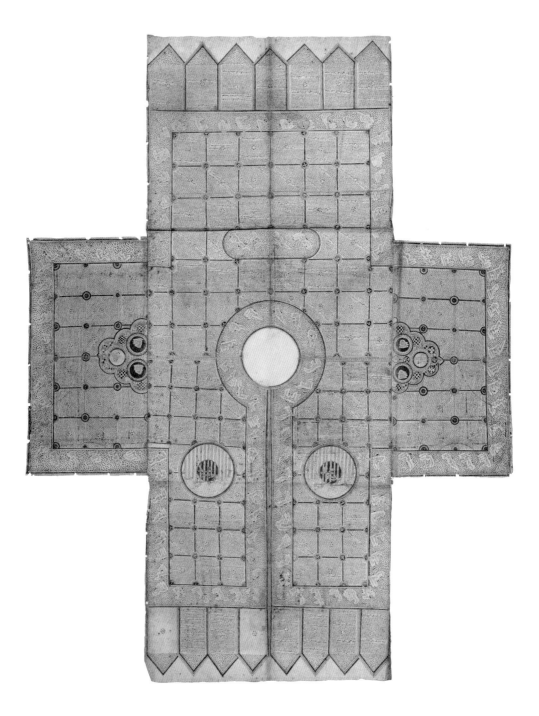

Divination pages

These pages are a particularly detailed example of a kind of material often found in devotional pocket books. On the left is a page with pious invocations, set out in a geometrical pattern underneath a statement acknowledging the supreme rule of Allah and the authority of his prophet Muhammad. The geometrical pattern of the page is thought to strengthen the effectiveness of the invocations on the entire page. The outer ring counter-clockwise from the top has the names of prominent prophets from the Qur'ān, starting with 'Isa (Jesus), then Musa (Moses), then Ibrahim (Abraham), and then Muhammad. In the four corners of the inner field of the page are the names of the first four caliphs, Abu Bakr, 'Umar, 'Uthman and 'Ali. These invocations are joined on the right-hand page by prayers to spiritual beings similar to angels or demons, known to Muslims as *jinn*—'genies', in the popular imagination.

MS. Laud Or. 184 fol. 1v, 2r; Divination pages from a devotional selection book; pre-18th/12th century.

Pocket book of Qur'ān selections

The last manuscript in this book is a devotional volume of modest quality. It is included as an example of the normal expression of an ordinary Muslim's relationship with the Qur'ān. Separate from the large, ornate luxury Qur'āns, or scholarly annotated editions that contains various textual variants, this is a simple devotional book to be carried on the person and treasured, turned to in times of trouble, and trusted for divine protection in a hostile world. This is what would have been carried by clerks, merchants, workman, seamen or soldiers. The content of this book consists of three surahs, the ninety-nine names of Allah and some prayers. The surahs are *Sūrat Yā Sīn*, 36; *Sūrat al-Ṣāffāt*, 'Those Ranged in Ranks', 37; and *al-Kāfirūn*, 'The Disbelievers', 109. These three are often found in these collections and are thought to have a special protective effect.

MS. Laud. Or. 15 fol. 3v, 4r; Pocket book of Qur'ān selections; *Sūrat al-Fātihah* (The Opening), 1:1–7; pre-18th/12th century.

Quotations

p. 2   Frithjof Schuon, *Understanding Islam*, London: Mandela Books, 1965, p. 43.

p. 5   T.S. Eliot, 'The Dry Salvages', *Four Quartets*, V, l. 17.

p. 5   Hadith Qudsi ('Holy Hadith') are traditions containing what are thought to be the words of Allah reported by Muhammad that are not contained in the Qur'ān. This one is from the collection made by Badii'uzzaman Furuzanfar, his *Aḥadith-I Mathnawi*, Tehran University, 1955/1334.

p. 39   Ya'qub b. Ishaq al-Kindi (d. 873/260), cited in Ibn Nadim's *Fihrist*, Dodge's translation, 1:19.

p. 61   Muhammad Ibn Ishaq al-Nadim, *The Fihrist: A Tenth Century* AD *Survey of Islamic Culture*, trans. Bayard Dodge, Chicago: Kazi Publications, 1998, 1:18.

p. 137 *A Winter in Arabia*, London: John Murray, 1945, p. 67.

Recommended reading

THE QUR'ĀN IN ENGLISH TRANSLATION

A.J. Droge, *The Qur'ān: A New Annotated Translation*. Sheffield: Equinox, 2013.

M.A.S. Abdel Haleem, trans., *The Qur'an*. Oxford: Oxford University Press, 2008.

ARABIC CALLIGRAPHY AND QUR'ĀNS

Sheila S. Blair, *Islamic Calligraphy*. Edinburgh: Edinburgh University Press, 2006.

Alain George, *The Rise of Islamic Calligraphy*. London: Saqi Books, 2010.

Nassar Mansour, *Sacred Script: Muhaqqaq in Islamic Calligraphy*. London: I.B. Tauris, 2011.

Annemarie Schimmel, *Calligraphy and Islamic Culture*. London: I.B. Tauris, 1990.

QUR'ĀN MANUSCRIPTS

Colin F. Baker, *Qur'an Manuscripts: Calligraphy, Illumination, Design*. London: British Library, 2007.

Manijfeh Bayani, *The Decorated Word: Qur'ans of the 17th to 19th Centuries*. London: Khalili Collections, 2009.

François Déroche, *Islamic Codicology: An Introduction to the Study of Manuscripts in Arabic Script*. London: Al-Furqan Heritage Foundation, 2005.

———— *The Abbasid Tradition: Qur'ans of the 8th to 10th Centuries A D*. London: Khalili Collections, 2006.

———— *Qur'ans of the Umayyads: A First Overview*. Leiden: Brill, 2014.

Duncan Haldane, *Islamic Bookbindings in the Victoria and Albert Museum*. London: World of Islam Festival Trust, 1983.

David Lewis James, *After Timur: Qur'ans of the 15th and 16th Centuries A D*. London: Nour Foundation with Oxford University Press, 1992.

———— *The Master Scribes: Qur'ans of the 11th to 14th Centuries A D*. London: Khalili Collections, 2006.

Martin Lings, *Qur'anic Art of Calligraphy and Illumination*. London: World of Islam Festival Trust, 1976.

Keith E. Small, *Textual Criticism and Qur'ān Manuscripts*. Portsmouth: Lexington Books, 2012.

THE BODLEIAN LIBRARY'S ARABIC COLLECTIONS

Robert Jones, 'Piracy, War, and the Acquisition of Arabic Manuscripts in Renaissance Europe', in *Manuscripts of the Middle East* 2. Leiden: Ter Lugt Press, 1987, pp. 96–110.

Colin Wakefield, 'Arabic Manuscripts in the Bodleian Library: The Seventeenth-Century Collections', in G.A. Russell, ed., *The 'Arabick' Interest of the Natural Philosophers in Seventeenth-Century England*. Leiden: Brill, 1994.

—— 'The Arabic Collections in the Bodleian Library', in Emilie Savage-Smith, *A New Catalogue of Arabic Manuscripts in the Bodleian Library, University of Oxford*, Volume I: *Medicine*. Oxford: Oxford University Press, 2011.

Acknowledgements

THERE ARE MANY PEOPLE WHO MAKE A BOOK LIKE THIS POSSIBLE. I would like to thank first of all Alasdair Watson, Bahari Curator of Persian Collections and Curator of Middle Eastern and Islamic Collections at the Bodleian Library, for opening the Bodleian's Qur'ān collection to me and for his generous assistance in research into the history of these manuscripts. Thanks also go to my editor Janet Phillips, and Samuel Fanous, Head of Bodleian Publishing (who suggested the idea for this book)—both have been a joy to work with. Thanks also go to friends Najib Bajali and Roy Michael McCoy III for their assistance with research. Most of all I'd like to thank my wife Celeste for her support and encouragement through the process of research and writing.

Special thanks are due to the David Collection of Copenhagen, Denmark, who from their collection of Islamic art have supplied images of one of their treasured manuscripts: a page from what is widely recognized as perhaps the oldest Qur'ān manuscript in existence.

Some significant contributions to this book were made by Dr Francesca Leoni, Yousef Jameel Curator of Islamic Art at the Ashmolean Museum of Art and Archaeology, Oxford University. Dr Leoni provided the captions for the eight Qur'ān manuscripts pictured in this book that are from the Ashmolean's collection. She also provided the description of the Ashmolean's Qur'ān manuscript collection in the introductory chapter. Our discussions provided me with valuable insights concerning the devotional use of Qur'ān texts and manuscripts which enhanced the text and captions of the final chapter.

Index of manuscripts

References to illustrations are in red

Index